THE SANJAY STORY

Vinod Mehta (1942–2015) left home with a BA third-class degree, experimented with a string of jobs, including that of a factory hand in suburban Britain, before accepting an offer to edit *Debonair*. He went on to become one of India's most influential editors, launching a number of successful publications, from the *Sunday Observer* to *Pioneer* to *Outlook*. Vinod Mehta has authored a biography of Meena Kumari, *Meena Kumari: The Classic Biography* (2013), and published (in 2001) a collection of his articles under the title *Mr Editor, How Close Are You to the PM?* His much-acclaimed memoir, *Lucknow Boy*, was published in 2011.

AF730121

THE SANJAY STORY

Vinod Mehta

HarperCollins *Publishers* India

First published in 1978 by Jaico Publishing

First published in hardback in India by
HarperCollins Publishers India, Cyber City, Building 10-A, Gurugram,
Haryana-122002, India
www.harpercollins.co.in

First published in paperback in 2015

2 4 6 8 10 9 7 5 3

Copyright © Vinod Mehta 1978, 2012, 2015

P-ISBN: 978-93-5177-387-0
E-ISBN: 978-93-5029-939-5

The views and opinions expressed in this book are the author's own and the facts are as reported by him, and the publishers are not in any way liable for the same.

Vinod Mehta asserts the moral right to be identified as the author of this work.

All rights reserved. No part of this publication may be reproduced, stored in a retrieval system, or transmitted, in any form or by any means, electronic, mechanical, photocopying, recording or otherwise, without the prior permission of the publishers.

Without limiting the exclusive rights of any author, contributor or the publisher of this publication, any unauthorized use of this publication to train generative artificial intelligence (AI) technologies is expressly prohibited. HarperCollins also exercise their rights under Article 4(3) of the Digital Single Market Directive 2019/790 and expressly reserve this publication from the text and data-mining exception.

Typeset in 11/14 Weiss
InoSoft Systems Noida

Printed and bound at
MicroPrints India, New Delhi

MIX
Paper
FSC FSC® C218906

This product is made of FSC®-certified and other controlled material.

HarperCollins Publishers, Macken House, 39/40 Mayor Street
Upper, Dublin 1, D01 C9W8, Ireland

For Sanjay

Contents

Introduction to the New Edition

MY BIOGRAPHY OF SANJAY Gandhi, *The Sanjay Story*, priced at Rs 35 in hardback, appeared in January 1978. It was a small critical and commercial success even though my version of the 'extra constitutional authority' came at a time when a succession of quickies, as they were dubbed, were keeping the nation alarmed and entertained by their sordid and comic revelations. The Emergency quickies, including those by Kuldip Nayar, the late Janardhan Thakur and Uma Vasudev, as Katherine Frank noted in *The Life of Indira Gandhi*, 'ran the gamut from the barely literate innuendos and gossip to polished intellectual assaults. Indira (and Sanjay) bashing was not only safe but also intellectually fashionable.' My quickie set out to be objective, but in that highly charged atmosphere, objectivity was in no great demand. It suffered a further infirmity. Sanjay refused to cooperate in the writing of the biography, insisting on copy-approval. It was an offer I had to refuse.

In 1978, my day job consisted of revamping *Debonair*. I was taking my first tentative steps into journalism-editorship, and while most of my creative energy was taken up with luring nubile girls to shed their clothes for Rs 250, *Debonair* (being a monthly magazine) allowed me time to investigate the person who, even in the opinion of his elder brother, had much to answer for. 'I will never forgive Sanjay for having brought mummy to this position,' Rajiv told family friend Pupul Jayakar.

Uncharitable critics describe what happened on 23 June 1980 as divine intervention. On this day, Sanjay perished in an avoidable plane crash. He was piloting the aircraft and it crashed barely 500 metres behind 12 Willingdon Crescent in New Delhi, the house where the Gandhis lived. In some sense, it was the chronicle of an accident foretold. Not only was the novice pilot given to flashy daredevilry and dangerous low-flying, which civil aviation authorities at the Delhi Flying Club had warned Indira about, he also insisted on wearing Kolhapuri chappals in the cockpit. Rajiv had repeatedly warned Sanjay to wear proper shoes and not chappals while flying. Characteristically, he paid no heed to the advice.

On the day the accident occurred, Sanjay was unusually excited. The Delhi Flying Club had recently acquired the advanced Pitts S-2A aircraft and Sanjay was itching to get inside it. Clad in kurta-pyjama and Kolhapuri chappals, he indulged in reckless manoeuvres. At 7.25 a.m. the plane crashed. Someone who lived close to 12 Willingdon Crescent was quoted in the press as asking her husband, 'Why is this plane flying so low?' Sanjay died instantly. It took eight surgeons four hours to stitch up his mutilated body.

Between the publication of my biography and the fatal accident, there is a gap of just over two years. What was Sanjay's life like in that interval? Certainly not short of drama, certainly not short of vituperative slander and certainly not without a few morsels of good news.

A commission under the former Supreme Court Chief Justice J.C. Shah had been appointed in 1977. Its official mandate was 'to enquire into subversion of lawful processes and well-established conventions, administrative procedure and practice, abuse of authority, misuse of powers, excesses and/or malpractices committed during the Emergency'. Sanjay had to appear before the commission almost every second day. Simultaneously, the Khanna Commission was set up to probe the numerous transgressions in Maruti Limited.

The Shah and Khanna commissions quickly descended into farce with both mother and son challenging and mocking the very existence of the commissions, saying they were unconstitutional and illegal. Justice Shah and Khanna were no match for them. Frequently, at Patiala House in Delhi, from where the Shah Commission operated, Sanjay was greeted by catcalls and abuse. Occasionally, his supporters and hostile spectators hurled steel chairs and physically assaulted each other. Heavy police bandobust was required to keep the peace.

In May 1978, Sanjay was sentenced to thirty days' imprisonment in Tihar Jail. Indira Gandhi told her wayward son as he entered jail, 'Don't lose heart, this is going to be your rebirth.'

While Sanjay and Indira were fighting legal battles in court, at home the two brothers and the two wives were barely on speaking terms. Relations between Rajiv and Sanjay were always 'chilly' and between Sonia and Maneka 'frigid'. Indira Gandhi sought to remain neutral, desperately trying to maintain some semblance of family peace. One morning, B.K. Nehru and his wife Flori were breakfasting with the Gandhis. 'Sanjay went into a rage and threw his plate across the room when Sonia failed to cook his eggs in the precise way he had ordered.' Indira did not say a word to Sanjay.

In January 1980, Indira Gandhi won back power from the Janata clowns, who gifted her the prime minister's chair meekly. Morarjee Desai led the strange cocktail which had dethroned Indira. Instead of concentrating on governance, they set out to 'punish' their nemesis by hook or by crook. This publicly stated goal was combined with vicious infighting. It would be fair to say the Janata leaders fell on their own swords with great facility.

Indira Gandhi stood and won from two constituencies, Raebareilly and Medak; Sanjay was elected comfortably from Amethi. With mother and son back to power, furious speculation raged in early 1980 as to what role the mother had planned for her son. Also, whether both had absorbed the egregious lessons of the Emergency – primarily excesses in the family planning and slum clearance programmes. Would a measure of civility replace the dreaded midnight knock in public life?

Indira Gandhi admitted some excesses might have been committed by sycophants and overzealous ministers, bureaucrats and assorted flunkeys, but her son, she insisted, was innocent and not involved. She characterized the excesses as 'gross exaggerations' spread by the media and long-standing Congress enemies. This defence repeated ad-nauseam suggested that Sanjay and his merry men would resume from where they had left off. Privately, Indira conceded the no-smoke-without-fire hypothesis, i.e., must be some truth in the sundry allegations. But her formal position was to live in denial.

On 31 March 1980, Maneka gave birth to a son. He was named Varun. Indira was over the moon. Now, she had three grandchildren, one from her problem son. Alas, Varun's birth did not ease the tensions between the brothers and their respective wives. Rajiv and Sonia retreated into their private space. It was as if they were hermetically sealed from the hectic goings-on at India's most politically active house.

If you are a devotee of what-if games, savour the following. What if Sanjay had survived the crash? Is it possible that Rajiv would have remained a private citizen with the younger brother carrying the dynastic torch forward? What if Maneka had not quarrelled so bitterly with her mother-in-law over who should inherit Sanjay's position as heir-apparent, and what if Maneka had not been thrown out at the midnight hour from Willingdon Crescent on the charge of publicly defying her mother-in-law and encouraging anti-party activities. (She formed her own group of Sanjay loyalists who began campaigning loudly for her to move into the vacancy created by Sanjay's death.) Would Maneka be playing the role Sonia is playing now?

And what of young Varun? Without what seems to be a permanent estrangement, would Varun have joined the BJP – a party in which he is a spectacular misfit? Would Varun be where Rahul is, if the two families had not split? From time to time reports surface of Varun having negotiated a return to the Congress. Till date that happy event has eluded the

Pilibhit MP. The verbal firecrackers Varun periodically lets off are intended to remind the Congress and the nation that Indira Gandhi had two grandsons, not one. With the BJP understandably eager to exploit Varun's surname and set up a cockfight between Rahul and Varun, Maneka's son seems like the dangling man. I think it is fair to assume there will be no change in his political status in the foreseeable future.

How will history remember Sanjay Gandhi? With the benefit of hindsight, I predict history will generally ignore him. It will treat him as a minor aberration, a blip on the screen of Indian public life. Mostly, he will be snubbed. A couple of lines or a couple of footnotes may be assigned to him – and they will range from the scathing to the platitudinous. Winston Churchill once said he was sure history would judge him kindly 'because I intend to write it'. Sanjay had no such option; losers never do. Not having left any record, much less justifications, for his extra-constitutional role in the Emergency, he has to rely on the assessment of professional historians – who till date have been unforgiving.

Doubtless, in any biography or evaluation of Indira Gandhi he will find mention as the son who led his mother astray. In our otherwise robust republic, the astray factor is a frequent visitor. The 'blind spot' syndrome, wherein an otherwise intelligent politician refuses to hear anything negative about her son or daughter, occurs again and again in our dynastic culture.

Sanjay, nevertheless, still has a few admirers. Khushwant Singh is an unrepentant fan. He sees Sanjay as the 'man who got things done'. The story could be apocryphal, but at the beginning of the Emergency, Indira is reported to have commended her younger son for making, among other things, 'the trains run on time'. Not surprisingly, Sanjay had no use for those who argued about means being as important as ends. The henchmen and henchwomen selected to carry out his orders were given a totally free hand as long as desired 'results' were achieved. Occasionally, the results were grossly exaggerated, sometimes they bordered on fiction.

Till very recently, the Congress had enormous difficulty in either disowning or owning Sanjay. The imposition of the Emergency was an easier evil to deal with. Though JP was apportioned part of the blame for forcing Indira's hand, the party accepted responsibility, making sure to emphasize the brevity of the eighteen-month period it lasted. And how it was Indira Gandhi who courageously took the decision against her son's advice to revoke it. Sanjay and his diabolical activities in that period, however, posed a trickier legacy to repudiate. With Maneka and Varun safely out of the party, the strategy adopted was studied and sustained silence. It worked to a certain extent.

As his only biographer (the quickies mentioned earlier all concentrated on the Emergency), I can state that the country may have forgotten Sanjay but it has not forgotten the Emergency. Has it made the right choice? Absolutely. The Emergency was unquestionably the bigger evil.

Living in denial, nevertheless, made life a tightrope walk for the Congress. In 2010 the tightrope was finally brought down. The party, with restrained fanfare, published its 'official history'. The editor was the no-nonsense Pranab Mukherjee. For the first time the party at once acknowledged and censured Sanjay for his controversial role in the Emergency. The *Times of India* in its report on the official history stated: 'The Congress has all but disowned Sanjay Gandhi, blaming the excesses committed during the Emergency in 1975 on his overzealous promotion of family planning and slum clearance programmes. This rare assessment of the Emergency and the person responsible for the popular anger against it has come in the party's official history.'

This is what the official history says, 'Vast sections of the population welcomed it (Emergency) initially since general administration improved. But civil rights activists took exception to the curbs on freedom of expression and personal liberties.' And now here is the crunch: 'Unfortunately, in certain spheres over-enthusiasm led to compulsion in enforcement of certain programmes like sterilization and clearance of slums.' After thirty-five years, the Congress bit the bullet. It was able to shake off the Sanjay albatross around its neck.

In this biography, I have tried to give the reader a flavour of the man who would be king. The man who almost captured the crown, had it not been for those damned Kolhapuri chappals.

October 2012
New Delhi

Introduction to the Original Edition

'LOOK WHAT THAT BASTARD has done', said the wizened old Congress Party worker. We were among a crowd of 200 people semi-encircling one of the many election score-boards at Bahadur-shah Zafar Marg in Delhi. And what we were surveying—the Congress Party worker mournfully, the rest of the crowd jubilantly —was a seat-by-seat account of results which were subsequently to be dubbed 'the Congress debacle'—perpetrated, orchestrated and executed, in the view of the Congress Party worker, by 'that bastard', Sanjay Gandhi.

In the nation itself, as in other parts of the world where Indian politics was being seriously followed, the Congress Party worker's abusive arraignment was re-echoed, re-stated and confirmed. Disagreement was essentially a matter of degree. If Sanjay Gandhi was not *the* author of the Congress debacle, he was, without doubt, the principal writer of it. Debate and dissent on young Mr Gandhi's post-emergency activities was circumscribed within these constraints.

Like many journalists, I had made my way to Delhi around result day accompanied by a vague premonition that something big was about to turn up; that the something would be 'historic' or 'monumental' or 'revolutionary' was inconceivable to me then. A friend asked me before I left what I expected to achieve simply by 'being there'. 'You can', he observed, 'hear the results in Bombay too.'

He was, of course, right. But during the past 21 months Delhi had become such a horrendous, knock at night, rumour-infested, look-over-your-shoulder-before-you-speak city that, if nothing else, one expected to detect a change of air.

I knew if the Congress lost a few seats (this arithmetical juggling became the parlour game during the campaign season. Ironically, those who supported Janata wanted nothing more than a strong opposition i.e. Janata, so that the 2-party system could be established in India. I found this kind of support both dishonest and cowardly. If one supported Janata then one should, I argued, go the whole hog and vote it into power, not into opposition) the result would be an anti-climax. Even if Mrs Gandhi retained a strength around 240 that too would be an anti-climax. If, however, Congress lost... On such slender hopes did I depart for Delhi.

When the results did come in over the radio, upset piled on upset, one experienced two distinct and disparate emotions.

First, there was a fleeting sense of disbelief. Could it be true? Could a party thought to be politically invincible be vincible?

Could All India Radio be playing a cruel joke? And finally: 'Could the Nehrus lose?'

It didn't take long for reality to assert itself. One quickly realized that what was majestically unfolding was nothing less, nothing more than a people exercising their sovereign right to choose their government. For thirty years they had chosen one government, this time they were choosing another. It was left to sophisticates like Nirad C. Chaudhuri to conclude that the Congress rejection of the electorate amounted to 'the most remarkable event in Indian history since independence'.

The second emotion experienced was of release. I don't particularly like journalistic clichés, but for once 'a country caged for two years has been set free' was a fairly accurate reflection of national mood. Walking down Connaught Place, the night a Janata Party victory was assured, I saw scenes of festivity and merriment and celebration which were certainly unique in my lifetime. A *paanwala*, who was distributing free *paans*, told me he had seen nothing like this since '47.

If anyone had doubts that the situation had changed, he was quickly reassured. On 21 March, when the Emergency was lifted, the Rajdhani arrived four hours late, L.I.C. workers in Kanpur came out on their usual lunch time morcha, a fist fight broke out in the dormant Press Club of Delhi, two family planning vans were burned in Calcutta, dancing school ads reappeared in the evening papers of Bombay, the price of smuggled scotch came down by 10 rupees. There was no mistaking it. Normalcy had returned to the country.

Along with normalcy, the horror stories started creeping out, first cautiously then with the momentum of an avalanche. Whole villages surrounded at night in pursuit of sterilization victims; bustees bulldozed at 24 hours notice; Chief Ministers toppled; bribery, corruption, nepotism; illegal imprisonment, tax raids, promotions, demotions, transfers, retirements; police torture, firing, even murder. All the conceivable evils associated with the body politic, it appeared, flourished at a time when we were supposedly 'marching to a better tomorrow'.

Naturally, the Congress Party quickly forwarded a euphemism for all their misdeeds, and the word they coined was not only inadequate, it was also ambiguous and effete. Thus 'excesses' entered the vocabulary of Indian polity. It was a word which in the months to come would bedevil the Congress Party for a long time.

Immediately, however, it would bedevil Sanjay Gandhi. Hardly a day passed when a new Sanjay scandal did not surface. According to the lately-freed press and according to those sniffing in and around the corridors of power, he was the sole architect of all or at least of most of the excesses. A similar point was made by some brave souls during the fag end of the Emergency— but obliquely. No one dared accuse Indira Gandhi's son by name. Instead, the accusation was made against the 'Extra Constitutional Authority'. (One of the few joys of political journalism in India is arcane phraseology. I have searched diligently and devoutly for the author of Extra Constitutional Authority, but he has resolutely escaped me.) Once the Congress lost, the subterfuge was no longer required and Sanjay was publicly and vociferously accused.

In the course of this book I hope we can discover the exact nature and dimensions of Sanjay's guilt. There are a few who believe that a witch-hunt is on against mother and son—especially against the son. There are more who believe he should be in jail.

Witch-hunt or jail? The polarity of the charge, if nothing else, asks for a careful response. It is necessary, therefore, to begin at the beginning and explore Sanjay's early life, explore what sociologists call the 'environmental structure' of his formative years. What was his home life like? How did he get on at school? What sort of a child was he? Was he closely attached to any member of his family? Did he understand his ancestral eminence? Cumulatively, this data might help explain the chemistry of his personality which in turn might help explain his later motivations and convictions.

In order to begin that kind of enquiry, one has first to enquire into the lives of two people who more than anyone else contributed to creating the kind of person Sanjay is today. Those two people are Feroze Gandhi and Indira Priyadarshini Nehru.

The Nehrus of Anand Bhavan

ALLAHABAD, TODAY, HAS NOTHING but a past. It is a small, boring, 'sleepy little town' which seems quite content with long-term somnolence. By some curious artistic mishap, the mercurial Urdu poet Firaq Gorukhpuri finds himself a citizen there. Otherwise the city needs a judge to disqualify a reigning prime minister from holding electoral office, or, alternatively, it needs a kumbh mela to attract attention. In between, Allahabad's claim to fame rests on its guavas.

Not so around the end of the nineteenth century. Then Allahabad was the capital of Uttar Pradesh (then known as North West Provinces); it was the legal metropolis of India; it was, along with Lucknow, one of the cultural show-places of the country; it was the centre of the printing press business in North India.

But, perhaps, the tallest feather in Allahabad's cap was the university. Year after year it produced academically brilliant graduates who were immediately absorbed into the then most prestigious profession—the I.C.S. More than half the Indian recruits into the civil service in 1931 were from Allahabad.

A visitor to the city around that period would probably have noticed a small group of wide-eyed men and women straining their necks outside a house on 1, Church Road. Although large trees obscured direct vision, the splendour and grandeur was still visible.

It was rumoured that inside there were '37 rooms' and 'spacious lawns, gardens of fruit, sparkling fountains, swimming pools, tennis courts, horses, carriages and a retinue of servants.' More: kennels for imported dogs, running water, electricity, Persian carpets, rich china and a car. Religious sanctity was provided by the belief that the house stood at the site on which 'Ram and Bharat met when the former returned from his 14 years of exile'.

The mansion—you couldn't possibly call it a house—was called 'Anand Bhavan' and its master was an affluent and extremely successful Kashmiri Brahmin lawyer called Motilal Nehru. With his son, daughters, brothers, sisters and nephews he lived under one roof in the best tradition of the Hindu joint family system.

Motilal, for half his life at least, was something of a prig. Like many 'natives' of his generation he mercilessly mimicked the English. He pursued a lifestyle which was commensurately extravagant (a journalist, Nihal Singh, presents the following menu list of a dinner in Anand Bhavan. 'The meals were good enough to be placed before royalty. Wine flowed liberally—wine of many kinds. With the dessert were brought boxes of cigars and cigarettes and liqueurs. A fair-sized bar could have been opened with the decanters placed in front of us.') and, more important, English. His suits were made in Saville Row and some said he sent them to London for washing; he drank only wines and imported spirits; he entrusted his children's education and care to English governesses. The point made by many of Motilal's biographers that he was an epicurean is only partly correct. He was an epicurean no doubt, but of the *vilayati* brand. (Invited to attend the durbar given by George V in Delhi, he had his attire especially rigged up in London for the occasion.)

No wonder then that Motilal's only son, Jawaharlal, modelled himself initially on his father. However, when it came to selecting a wife for his son, the father preferred an arranged match—the single most important attribute of the bride being her physical fitness. Since Motilal had suffered on account of his own wife's constant ill-health, he was determined to find for his son a girl of sound limb and body. He made a disastrous choice.

Although there were many nubile girls possessing sound limb and body, and although some of them satisfied caste considerations, Motilal had to do some searching. Like all fathers he was looking for the impossible amalgam: beauty and brains, wealth and refinement. And naturally he didn't find it. Eventually he compromised and settled for a 17 year old Delhi maiden called Kamala Kaul.

Kamala, by all accounts, was beautiful—nevertheless, by Motilal's standards her brains, refinement and wealth fell short by varying degrees. Wealth and brains were not in short supply in Anand Bhavan, so Kamala needed coaching only in one sphere— refinement. After all, Motilal entertained Sirs, Governors, Judges, I.C.S. Officers, Collectors while his future daughter-in-law spoke broken English and didn't quite know how to handle a knife and fork.

An extraordinary solution was agreed on. Motilal persuaded Kamala's father to allow his daughter to stay at Anand Bhavan before the nuptials so that she could pick up the necessary social graces from his famous English governesses. In this manner, a bride was made ready for Jawaharlal and by early February 1916 training was complete. Kamala was pronounced fit for entry into the Nehru portals.

The marriage was formally solemnized in Delhi with suitable pomp and show. 'Four months preparations had been going on ... Jawahar made a handsome bridegroom and Kamala was one of the loveliest brides I have ever seen,' recollects Krishna, Motilal's daughter.

Twenty-one months after the marriage, Kamala produced her first and only child (there was another birth but the baby, a boy, lived only two days).[1] On 19 November 1917, Kamala gave birth to a 'puny female child weighing four pounds'. The grandmother appeared sexually disappointed, 'Oh, but it should have been a boy.' Reprimand came quickly from Motilal: 'You must not say such a thing, even think of it. This daughter of Jawahar, for all you know, may prove better than a thousand sons.'

In the christening parents and grand-parents were simultaneously involved. Indira was Motilal's choice, Priyadarshini was Jawaharlal's. The jointly conceived name meant 'dear to behold'.

Understandably, the expectation was that 'in this house of great wealth Indira was to find great love.' Certainly the

---

1 Ruskin Bond mentioned this fact in his book on Nehru commissioned by Dr Karan Singh for the Nehru Trust. It was deleted.

external trappings of great love were abundantly present. Motilal ordered a pram from Calcutta for his dear Indu and generally smothered her with creature comforts—but that, as any school child psychologist will tell you, is not enough.

Anand Bhavan was not a family home, it was the forum of an embryonic national independence movement. Here the first Joint Congress-Muslim League met, here the foundation of the Non-Cooperation movement was laid by Mahatma Gandhi, here the All-Parties Conference met to draw up a Constitution for India, here the Nehru Report demanding immediate Dominion Status was drafted. When these momentous events were not taking place, Indira's home was usually silent, almost in partial mourning: the men were in jail.

Even if Anand Bhavan had been de-politicized it would still have been poor breeding ground. Motilal was a good old-fashioned male chauvinist imbued with a Victorian sense of discipline (he once beat his son 'blind with pain' for removing a pen from his study). Though they turned out to be scarcely less remarkable later on, in Anand Bhavan the Nehru women were expected to be mere appendages of the men, not exactly barefoot, pregnant and in the kitchen, but their place and position was immovably fixed.

Could Indira have turned to her mother for love? Possibly, but Kamala herself was suffering from the intense neglect and humiliation she suffered in the lofty Nehru home.

There was first the stigma of not really being worthy of the great family she had entered. Kamala bitterly resented her earlier 'training' based on the assumption that she was ignorant of the finer (westernized) points of life. There was also some Hindi film type trouble between Kamala and the other women members of the Nehru household, particularly Vijaya Lakshmi.

All this would have been bearable for Kamala had Jawaharlal been a concerned and loving husband. But he was preoccupied with his rising political star and would accept no domestic interruptions. On one occasion, when Kamala was ill, Jawaharlal had to attend a political rally. As he was leaving Kamala suddenly fainted. Jawaharlal picked her up, put her on the couch, called the maid, pondered for a moment, and left. In fact, it became clear very early that he obtained little companionship from his wife. On his honeymoon in Kashmir he left his young bride in Srinagar and went off with a cousin on a two week trek.

Kamala, it should be pointed out, was neither banal nor boring. She was intelligent, proud, optimistic, attractive, sensitive and quick-witted. Minoo Masani remembers other qualities: 'A wonderful person, warm, kind and considerate. You couldn't help admiring her.' J. P., who came into contact with her while working in the Allahabad AICC office, considers her 'the noblest member of the Nehru family whose passing away robbed it of an indefinable quality of the spirit that never returned to the family again'. Unfortunately all these aspects were never recognized by Jawaharlal or others in Anand Bhavan. So how could a lonely daughter find cheer with a lonely mother?

Despite the enormous love and affection that existed between Indira and her father, she never forgave him for the way he treated her mother. Indira saw Kamala languishing daily under callous neglect. It must be said in Jawaharlal's defence that he did acknowledge his neglect posthumously: 'She (Kamala) must have suffered...an unkindness to her would almost have been better than this semi-forgetful attitude.'

Kamala for her part slid progressively into introspection

and silence. She suffered eloquently, quietly, uncomplainingly. (Did this have any effect on her lungs? I spoke to two doctors, both however refused to commit themselves. All they would say is that depression could be a 'contributory cause' for T.B.) And it is from Kamala that Indira inherited her now famous ability to recoil within herself and freeze, thus forming a protective covering against intrusions into non-political life. Soon after her mother's death in Switzerland, Indira said, 'I saw her being hurt, and I was determined not to be hurt.'

THERE WERE NOT MANY Parsee families living in Allahabad in those days. One of the few were the Gandhis. They were middle-class, professional, housed in a modest bungalow not far from Church Road. The main provider was a Bombay naval officer who, because of the nature of his job, sent his sons and daughters to live with his sister in Allahabad. She was a surgeon of some repute, nonetheless not very rich. Among the sons sent for care was a two-year-old Feroze, the youngest in the family.

Feroze went to school in Allahabad, and later in the university there he enrolled for an L.L.B. degree. It was through this connection that he wormed his way into Anand Bhavan, for it was Motilal's practice to invite promising young students over to his house. But Feroze didn't pay much attention to either law or Motilal, he paid attention to Kamala and Indira—in that order.

His devotion to Kamala remains something of a mystery. Of course she must have shown her characteristic concern and kindness for the young lad, and he on his part may have sympathized with her crucifying loneliness. Or perhaps he succumbed to Kamala's quiet charisma. Or as Krishna put it, 'Feroze's fondness for Kamala was romantic'. Once, while Jawaharlal was in Naini Jail, some miscreants put up ugly posters in Allahabad insinuating an affair between Kamala and young Feroze. Someone anonymously sent one of these posters to Nehru and he was furious. Being an intelligent man he did not question either Kamala or Feroze, but he did ask Rafi Ahmed Kidwai to investigate the poster slander. Minoo Masani remembers how at breakfast one morning at Anand Bhavan, when Feroze's name was mentioned, Nehru asked abruptly: 'Minoo, can you imagine anyone falling in love with my wife?' Masani replied quickly: 'Yes. In fact I could fall in love with her myself.'

Whatever the reason, by 1930 Feroze was a frequent visitor to Anand Bhavan, often in the company of Indira, but more often in the company of Kamala. He would help her in looking after and feeding Congress workers released from jail. Occasionally when Kamala had to visit adjacent villages to rehabilitate released workers Feroze would accompany her in the capacity of friend and waiter. He would carry her special diet.

But these were only minor manifestations of his devotion. 'Kamala received his attention and affection in even more generous measure in sickness. Owing to the highly contagious nature of her ailment, many near relations tended to avoid visiting Kamala at times when she was bed-ridden... Feroze showed no such hesitation or concern for his own health... He would not hesitate to do for her such an unpleasant task as cleaning her spittoon, a chore that even Anand Bhavan sweepers performed reluctantly and with unconcealed distaste.'

If you were young, gifted and even vaguely patriotic in the '30s, you were likely to be sucked into the prevailing political drama. And Feroze was no exception. Though in his case, the police did help.

One day Feroze was watching a peaceful morcha against the Simon Commission. The Commission had ostensibly come to India in order to suggest constitutional reforms; in reality it was a sop to militant nationalist opinion. As happens in most peaceful morchas there was police provocation, a couple of stones were hurled and then a full lathi charge. Watching from the sidelines, Feroze was caught in the ensuing melee and received many lathi blows. This was his political baptism.

Soon he joined the Congress in Allahabad and attached himself to K. D. Malaviya, then Secretary of the Allahabad Congress Committee. By 1933 a 21-year-old Feroze was a political veteran. He had taken part in countless agitations and, even more laudable, had been to jail three times.

Kamala's health, meanwhile, continued to deteriorate. The doctors recommended she go for treatment to Berlin and then to a sanitarium in Badenweiler, a health resort in Germany's picturesque Black Forest. Since Jawaharlal had other things on hand, Indira and a cousin of Kamala's were to accompany the patient. When Feroze got wind of this plan he made his own. He decided he would abandon nationalist politics for a few years and catch up with his studies—interrupted due to his extracurricular political activities—at the London School of Economics. He raised money from his aunt and it is said Kamala helped too. Thus while Indira and her mother made their way to Germany, Feroze made his way to London. As he had arrived mid-term he didn't get admission into L.S.E. immediately.

Waiting didn't bother him. Hardly had he arrived in London when he made the first of many visits to see Kamala at Badenweiler. He nursed her, read to her, cheered her. And when she died at the age of 37 in February 1936, there were at her bedside Jawaharlal, Indira and a doctor. 'Behind them in the background was a dutiful and devoted Feroze'.

With Kamala no more, Feroze's gaze turned full focus on Indira. Although Mrs Gandhi's biographers are unanimous that she was then a 'virginal pale faced beauty' (a dubious compliment at the best of times), photographic plates suggest an angular, shy, plain looking girl with the prominent 'Kashmiri' nose. Indira, now studying in London preparatory to joining Oxford, met Feroze frequently, and despite the fact that he courted her assiduously and conventionally—opera, ballet, theatre, restaurants—love took time.

Did he transfer his affections from mother to daughter? Perhaps. He also felt the daughter, now living alone in a London boarding house, needed looking after.[2] All of which explains Feroze's 'protective quality' which, as time went on, developed into something less protective.

Another man who helped love along was Krishna Menon.

Menon had pounced on England in 1924, and among the first things he did was to revitalize and rejuvenate an ailing organization purporting to advance India's case in Britain. Menon took 'The Commonwealth of India League' by the neck, fought with its elders, shortened the name to 'India League', and by 1931 he had made it into a bustling, dynamic, combative, unignorable, leftist propaganda platform for Indian

---

2 It is more than likely that Kamala too asked Feroze to keep an eye on Indira.

independence. Some of England's brightest names, including Harold Laski, Bertrand Russell, Aneurin Bevan, Fenner, Brockway, Lord Soper, Michael Foot, Barbara Castle, Sybil Thorndike, Jennie Lee, Kingsley Martin were all to become active members of Menon's 'India League' —and make no mistake, it was Menon's 'India League'. Everybody understood that.

Like most thinking Indians at that time in England, Feroze and Indira gravitated into Menon's fold. Besides India there were other causes: the rise of fascism in Europe, Spain, anti-semitism, China. True to its international credentials, the 'India League' was involved in all of them.

Soon all the spare time Feroze and Indira had was spent working for Menon. And he was to have a lasting ideological impact on both of them. For Feroze he was to become a lifelong, infallible guru. Indeed, one way of incurring Feroze's unremitting wrath was to criticize Menon. (The day he had his fatal heart attack Feroze was greatly troubled: in the Lok Sabha there had been a virulent attack on Menon.) For Indira, the impact was less permanent. (On the first day of the Bangladesh War a friend of mine had an appointment with Mrs Gandhi. He arrived 10 minutes early and found an anxious Menon trying to hustle a meeting. 'I've been waiting three days. Why don't you give up your meeting and let me see her instead?' he asked my friend. Just then Haksar came out and told Menon firmly that the Prime Minister was too busy. A weary Menon picked up his stick and left.) Nonetheless, it was while working for the 'India League' that the Feroze-Indira friendship took on romantic overtones.

It was a strange time to conduct a courtship. England was at war, Hitler threatened to eat up Europe, bombs were falling every night, rationing was on, lights were out by 6 p.m. Thus for Jawaharlal the paramount question was of his daughter's physical safety. Therefore when he heard that she was returning home he was not worried (unlike his sister Krishna who thought aeroplanes too dangerous) what mode of travel she adopted.

Actually she returned by sea. In late 1941 Indira took the good ship 'City of Paris' bound for India via the Cape of Good Hope. With her were two companions—Feroze and Bhupesh Gupta. And by the time the ship landed in Bombay, Feroze and Indira 'had made up their mind to marry'.[3]

They also decided that the formal 'asking' of the girl's father would be done by the girl, not by the boy. Indira, conscious of the many hurdles ahead, took upon herself the twin responsibility of popping the question and its timing.

Jawaharlal, meanwhile, was in District Jail, Dehradun, completely oblivious of his daughter's intentions and manoueverings. His intention was to have her near him, for which purpose he arranged a cottage in Mussoorie. Krishna was also invited up to the mountains.

Every fourteen days (visitors were allowed twice a month) Indira and Krishna would drive into Dehradun to cheer up the prisoner. Though desperate to air the big secret, Indira kept her peace. Indeed, she waited for Krishna to go back to Allahabad before she informed her father of her matrimonial intentions.

Jawaharlal was 'greatly upset'. He told her bluntly that he

---

3 Much later someone asked Feroze how he had managed to 'phasao' (ensnare) Indira into marriage. Feroze replied, 'In life if you try for anything long enough you get it'.

did not favour the proposal. He had, however, no wish to appear dictatorial. He suggested she consult her two aunts and ascertain their views on the subject.

The aunts were not in favour either, and they told her so unequivocally. Opposition was united and unyielding.

It must be pointed out that Jawaharlal, Krishna and Vijaya Lakshmi's objections to the match were thoroughly petty and unworthy of a family laying claims to intelligence, rationality, aristocracy and unorthodoxy. They were not objecting to the implication of 'love marriage', which it undoubtedly was. (Vijaya Lakshmi had a well publicized love affair, Krishna's was a love marriage, while a cousin, B. K. Nehru, had married a Hungarian Jew). They were not objecting to the inter-caste or inter-religious aspect. (Vijaya Lakshmi and Krishna's husbands were non-Kashmiris, Krishna's husband was even non-Brahmin; a cousin had wed a Muslim.) They were not objecting to Feroze's academic standing. (He had studied at no less an institution than the London School of Economics.) They were not objecting to Feroze as a person. (They had known him long enough and by all accounts liked him.)

What they were objecting to was quite simply Feroze's inferior social and financial status. Could this man of few means and even fewer prospects keep the comfort-loving, luxury-reared Indira in the manner she had been accustomed? That was one problem—the other was their dislike of gate-crashers.

Naturally, they didn't tell Indira that their opposition to Feroze was based on his unimpressive bank balance. Instead they told her all the things elders usually say when they want to dislocate a proposed marriage: you are too young, wait a while, see some other boys, be sure before you say yes...

Indira proved a worthy opponent to such diversionary tactics. She reminded her aunt Krishna: 'It took you only ten days to make up your mind about Rajabhai[4] and I have known Feroze for years. So why should I have to wait and why should I meet other young men?' Krishna had no reply.

A final impediment was erected. Jawaharlal said he agreed in principle, but would it not be proper to wait until his release? You couldn't have a wedding with your father in jail. The catch, as Jawaharlal knew, was the term of his imprisonment: he had spent only one out of a four-year sentence.

Indira was temporarily stumped—but not for long. On 14 December 1941, the British Government freed many political prisoners, including Jawaharlal. Now there were no impediments.

In all fairness, among the Nehru clan, Jawaharlal's objections to the marriage had tinges of honesty: he feared the alliance mismatched because of vastly dissimilar temperaments. (How right he was!) However, he had no evidence to substantiate his fears, and thus he was unable to bring up even obliquely the subject of incompatibility with a daughter crushingly in love.

At this stage, Mahatma Gandhi got into the act. Jawaharlal, keen on an outside opinion, requested Bapu to cast his expert eye on the pair.

Indira and Feroze were summoned, and Gandhi got, as he saw it, to the heart of the matter. In separate interviews he asked each partner whether they truly loved each other or was it just 'sexual infatuation'. No record is available of either partner's reply, however historians do confirm that Bapu

---

4 Krishna's husband.

was satisfied that carnality alone was not the motive for the marriage.

One impediment—a purely practical one—still remained. Since Feroze was a Parsee and Indira a Hindu Brahmin, the rituals of the ceremony had to be sorted out. The easiest thing would have been for Feroze to become a Hindu, but Jawaharlal was on record as opposing such conversions of convenience. In his view they were 'lies'.

Fortunately, there was at hand an ingenious pandit. Lachmi Dhar Shastri, a professor of Sanskrit, plundered the Vedas and produced a dubious sacrament which he claimed would be in accordance with the scriptures and also binding on people of differing faiths. Jawaharlal took the priest at his word.

On the morning of 26 March 1942 (Ram Naumi) Indira and Feroze were married. Prof. Shastri's ceremony was Vedic, tedious, novel and politicized. Indira had to hold a sword in one hand and warn: 'If there are any people in the four quarters of the earth who venture to deprive us of our freedom....'

A political wedding was, without doubt, patriotic and praiseworthy, but was it legal? The eminent lawyer Sir Tej Bahadur Sapru, a close friend of the Nehrus, had no doubts. Although the ceremony was performed by a recognized pandit and although it had the appearance of religious sanction 'it would not be able to stand test of a court'.

In his pictorial profile *Indira Gandhi*, G.D. Khosla claims that 'Feroze had gone through a conversion to Hindusim to lend conformity to orthodox views about Hindu laws; and to guard against any possible legal objection, the couple went through a form of civil marriage after a brief honeymoon in Kashmir'. Other biographers and observers confirm that Feroze did convert and a civil marriage did take place.

If it did, Indira was unaware of it. And so was Feroze. 'Certainly not', was Mrs Gandhi's emphatic response when she was questioned about Feroze's conversion and a subsequent civil marriage.

Thus when Mr and Mrs Feroze Gandhi departed for their honeymoon to Kashmir they were supremely happy, blissfully in love but not lawfully wedded man and wife![5]

Jawaharlal, understandably, found it difficult to accept the loss of his only child. For some time after the marriage he addressed mail to his daughter under the dual title Indira Nehru Gandhi—something which didn't please the husband very much.

FORT ROAD IN GEORGE Town, Allahabad was not far from Anand Bhavan. Here Feroze rented a small house for himself and his wife. He was now something of a photo-journalist with pronounced pro-Russian sympathies. In his spare time, he tended his small garden, built furniture and generally pottered around the house.

Tranquil domesticity was short-lived. In August that year Mahatma Gandhi launched the 'Quit India' movement and in one stroke brought the entire country to a standstill. Tens of thousands, including the top Congress leadership, were arrested. The Gandhis of Allahabad didn't lag behind and Indira had her first experience of tear gas and arrest. Both husband and wife were taken into custody while trying to hoist the tricolour at a meeting of college students. He was

---

5 In an interview with Uma Vasudev, Indira Gandhi said: 'It just didn't bother me whether it (her marriage) was legal or not'.

sentenced to twelve months imprisonment and a fine of Rs. 200; she was detained without trial.

The following year in May, Indira was released and three months later Feroze was set free. The couple went back to Allahabad and to political activity, albeit of a less hectic kind.

New Year 1944 brought news—both good and bad. Ranjit, Vijaya Lakshmi's husband, died and Indira discovered she was pregnant.

A son, Rajiv, was born on August 20. Jawaharlal, in prison and always fretting over his daughter's health, was delighted at the birth of a grandson, and even more delighted that 'Indu had an easy delivery'.

At this juncture in the lavishly documented life and times of Indira Gandhi, only Indira survives, Feroze becomes a footnote, a matrimonial accident. There is very little mention of him and even when he is resurrected it is only to record: 'Feroze came for breakfast', 'Feroze had a heart attack', 'Feroze improved', 'Indira rushed to the hospital'. Political and social chroniclers insist that all was well between the couple; only the demands of a fierce national struggle kept them apart. Even if this were true, Feroze's part in the fierce national struggle is conspicuously unrecorded, and even more crucial, there is an absence of even the slightest bit of domestic tittle-tattle.

Feroze's absence, however, is inadvertently emphasized. Since the books on Mrs Gandhi are legion and since most of them are pictorial, some telling portraits have crept in: Indira at the christening of her first son; Indira and kids on holiday in Kashmir; Indira with family at breakfast table; Indira and Rajiv on horseback; Indira, Rajiv, Sanjay on a ship. All these are normal, happy album pictures of a seemingly integrated family life. Curiously, the father of the family is always absent while the grandfather is usually present. One would almost imagine that Feroze had passed away.

Actually he was very much in circulation. He had shifted from Allahabad to Lucknow where he was managing a daily called *National Herald*. The *Herald* was a paper which Jawaharlal had started in 1938 to expound the nationalistic viewpoint, a rival to the *Pioneer* which unashamedly supported the British. It had a brilliant young editor in Chalapathi Rau who, like all brilliant young editors, knew everything about journalism but nothing about management and finance. The paper was in the red and it was Feroze's job to make it financially viable. He hit it off well with Chalapathi who remembers that they cooperated 'closely to produce some magnificent supplements. ... I had discovered and valued qualities in him which were to make him famous and known to the world later.'

If Feroze was professionally active, and if he and his wife were still 'very much in love' why, then, does he drop out? One must remember that most of the literature on Mrs Gandhi was written during her term of premiership. Writers knew, and if they didn't know they were promptly told, that the one area of her life which was taboo was her marital life. In this respect she herself set a fine example. In a book titled 'The Speeches and Reminiscences of Indira Gandhi' (the copyright, by the way, is held by one Indira Nehru Gandhi) which covers her activities from childhood to 1972, the name Feroze Gandhi appears twice. (A biographer of Mrs Gandhi told me some years ago how unhappy the Prime Minister was with the attention the writer had paid to the colour of her saree, the *tika* on her forehead, her honeymoon.) Mrs Gandhi obviously preferred reading about her political triumphs and vicissitudes rather than household gossip.

One can't blame her. By the end of 1947 the marriage showed signs of cracking up, and by 1952 it had cracked up. The reasons of the crack-up are, as one would expect, under-discussed. There are vague murmurings that 'Indira did not relish (Feroze's) extrovert, very informal and gay bohemian informality.' However, the reason most readily advanced encompasses the age-old Indian myth of sacrifice. Indira was required by her father, her father was required by the nation—so the brave and altruistic Indira sacrificed her dearest possession, her marriage, at the altar of national good. Indeed, it is suggested that Feroze very sportingly allowed the dissolution of his marriage, for he too was devoted to national good.

While these reasons sound plausible and patriotic, they are just the tip of the iceberg.

Incompatibility, of course, was what Jawaharlal feared even before he gave his daughter away. Certainly Feroze and Indira were not, in marriage counsellor terms, 'alike'. He was a robust, paan-chewing, gossip-spreading, fun-loving loquacious man, who despite his easy affability had serious views and convictions. His idea of a convivial evening was a gathering of half-a-dozen soft Marxists capable of producing witty and stimulating conversation, which he himself would frequently lead. Soft Marxist conversations being lengthy, they would go late into the night at which time a sumptuous non-Marxist meal was provided. Eating was one of Feroze's passions—perhaps the only Parsee characteristic remaining, otherwise for all practical purposes he was a naturalized Lucknowi—and whenever he was invited to dinner he would enquire after the menu and the qualifications of the chef.

Indira was demonstrably different. A private person, not given to public manifestations of emotion, she was reserved, careful, frail—not uninterested or timid or unhospitable, just shy. Indira couldn't—indeed had no wish to—compete with her husband when it came to verbal repartee. What she enjoyed was entertaining his friends and acting the gracious hostess, a role she played superbly later on.

This then is the sum total of the Indira-Feroze dispute. And as a cause for serious marital strife it sounds improbable. Successful marriages are not dependent on a complete identity of personality traits. Very often individuals with dissimilar interests and habits make enduring couples. Therefore a back-slapping and laughing Feroze could have been the ideal foil for a sensitive and sober Indira.

Mrs Gandhi has not said much about her marriage and she has said even less about the alleged incompatibility which wrecked her home. To one gutsy biographer, however, she did open up briefly and the explanation she offered was so incoherent and unintelligible that I can do no better than reproduce both question and answer in full:

'In what way would you say you and Feroze were incompatible?'

'Oh, I don't know—you have to pay for everything I suppose. You can't have everything. He (Feroze) couldn't have become what he did if he hadn't married me. If I had been a sweet little wife like anybody else he wouldn't have wanted to prove himself somehow. Perhaps I too would have been content to live a very domestic life and not even turn to politics.'

Along with temperamental incompatibility there appears to be sexual incompatibility. Because they had dissimilar temperaments their attitudes to sex were correspondingly dissimilar. Indira's attitude was based more on procreation; Feroze's was based more on the pleasure principle. Thus there was a kind of sexual conflict, but it must be pointed out that it was not unique. Most couples confront and solve problems of this nature.

Alas, Feroze also had 'an eye for a pretty face', 'an eye for beauty and its concomitant diversions' (Mrs Gandhi's biographers' better euphemisms) which didn't, one can be sure, please Indira very much. The first of a series of infidelities occurred in Lucknow when Feroze was managing the *National Herald*. In India, where biographers are exceedingly circumspect and respectful, one has to tread carefully or face charges of sexual sensationalism. Nonetheless, Feroze's interest in women (which, incidentally, Sanjay inherits) wasn't and isn't exactly a secret.

Although Feroze tried desperately hard to conduct his amorous adventures discreetly, he was constantly being caught out, not least by his wife. Jaffar, an old friend of Feroze, says: 'The more he would try to hide his affairs, the more they would come out. He was hopeless in managing this area of his life. He used to know a certain lady and I warned him he should not see her because she was obviously exploiting his name and friendship. He didn't listen to me. Then one day he came running. "Jaffar, you were right, that girl has got me into trouble. She was arrested in Paris. They say she is a Russian spy. In her testimony she has given my name. Now there is an enquiry against me!" Nothing I think finally happened, but this kind of mismanagement was very much a part of Feroze.'

On another occasion Jaffar found a bag of mangoes at Feroze's house. 'Don't touch those—they are for Pantjee,' said Feroze. That evening Jaffar went to the house of a lady. Feroze was also present. She brought out a bag of mangoes and Jaffar immediately said: 'Funny, I saw a similar bag of mangoes at Feroze's house. But of course they were for Pantjee.' There was an embarrassing silence. When the lady was out of earshot, Feroze said: 'Jaffar you always say the wrong thing at the wrong time.'

Altogether sexual incompatibility probably played a larger part in the Indira-Feroze unofficial divorce than temperamental incompatibility.

Another cause for incompatibility, though a minor one, was Nehru.

By 1947, he was a lonely man in a lonely job (remember Kennedy's remark about the American Presidency being the loneliest job in the world). After the turmoil of a 16-hour day he wanted the solace of a close relative. This was a perfectly normal expectation, but not a mandatory one. There are countless examples of political leaders who have led and are leading solitary lives. Mr Nehru would have survived his loneliness and made no worse or better a Prime Minister without his daughter's proximity. Meanwhile, the assertion that Nehru required Indira for social reasons, for entertaining the vast array of glittering guests who came regularly to visit him, is so ludicrous that it defies comment. One would think that secretaries, sisters, valets, servants did not exist.

Whatever Mr Nehru's private and social requirements, Indira's responsibility was to her husband and children. Indian wives, wives the world over, know that once they get married their first allegiance is to their new family.

But what do you do when you know your marriage is beyond repair, when you know that time will not heal, it will exacerbate? If you are the suffering Sita type you will endure a wretched life hoping for rewards in the next world. If, like Indira, you like your reward in this world, you break.

When she decided to more or less permanently move in with Jawaharlal in 1947, Indira had written off her marriage. And like all estranged wives she went running to her father's house—and stayed there. Perhaps this explanation is altogether too simplistic and prosaic, but it is more plausible and certainly more human than the one attributing 'sacrifice' and 'national good' for the break-up of the marriage.

Mummy's Boy

WHEN LADY AND SIR Stafford Cripps came to India in 1946 they came with separate ambitions.

Sir Stafford Cripps was part of a three-man Cabinet Mission exploring ways and means of handing over power. Clement Attlee, now leading a Labour Government in Britain, had instructed the Mission to establish a machinery of decision 'that would enable Indian leaders to receive political power in no way incompatible with the sovereign dignity of India'.

Lady Cripps, meanwhile, had come in search of a Kashmiri shawl; but she knew nothing about Kashmiri shawls. Therefore as a shopping guide she approached Indira, now living in Delhi with her father in a small bungalow on 17 York Road. Indira could easily have refused the invitation. Lady Cripps and her husband were not exactly friends of India—rather they represented a colonial power dragging its feet. The Nehrus, however, had a reputation for civility and friendship to white aliens. Lady Cripps further diluted any residual hostility by paying compliments to Indira's superior shawl sense.

The only problem in going was physical. Indira was over eight months pregnant and her English doctor was most disturbed with the way the pregnancy was progressing. Because of her marital woes, Indira appeared depressed, tired and tense. Nevertheless, on 13 December she did go shawl shopping with Lady Cripps and that evening there was a rare family re-union. Feroze had come from Lucknow, Mr Nehru for once was at home, Krishna, her husband and two sons had arrived from Bombay. 'We had a pleasant evening', remembers Krishna, 'Jawahar's witticisms brought a great deal of laughter and Indira was in fine form.' A good dinner was had by all.

Some time after midnight Indira's maid knocked on Krishna's door and woke up Feroze: Memsahib was having labour pains.

At 3 a.m. on a cold Delhi night, Feroze, Krishna, Indira and the maid drove to Willingdon Hospital. It was agreed that Jawaharlal should not be disturbed as he did not like waking up early. The English doctor, who had been informed by phone, went straight to the hospital and there he spent over six hours with his patient in the labour room. He was not helped in his task by Krishna and Feroze who had their own ideas on how the baby should be delivered.

Just before ten the next morning the doctor came out and announced the news. Indira had had a very difficult delivery; she had lost a great deal of blood. She had also at 9.27 a.m. given birth to a son, who was as well as could be expected in the circumstances.

Only the good news was communicated to Jawaharlal. He came immediately to the hospital and was alarmed to see how weak and pale his daughter had become. Indeed, as the doctor confirmed, in the process of producing her second child, Indira Gandhi had nearly lost her life.

The child, according to occidental astrology, was born under the sign of Sagittarius. Mr Leon Petulangro, an internationally renowned gipsy and writer of numerous books on Zodiac signs, states that a person born on 14 December would have 'insatiable curiosity, formidable aggression, acute observation, analysis and reason.' Further: 'fond of giving advice, popular and social.... naturally equipped for positions of authority... would excel in medicine or law or the church and make a good technical expert, nurse or matron.'

For more poignant and devastatingly inaccurate predictions one must turn to Mahraj Sharndas Udasi who prepared the said child's horoscope for the 15 August 1976 issue of the *Illustrated Weekly of India:* 'Sanjay Gandhi's rashi is Simha. The horoscope (kundali) is of Maker Lagna. The house is of the Sun. It denotes a proud, independent man who completes every project he starts and does not allow family or friends to alter or influence his decisions.

'The man born under these stars has the makings of a world political figure. One special achievement will catapult him to international renown. The highest political office could come between 1982 and 1985 or in March-April 1986. But he must be cautious about women. Election victory is ensured from February, 1977. Business ventures are not successful to start with. A newspaper business has good chances of doing well. There is good money in farming but not much in machinery.

'The man born under this sign has a marked interest in nature, poetry and religion. After 55 he could take to spiritualism and give up everything—political and personal...'

What sort of world was the boy born into? He would need only to look on to the lawns of his small house to catch a glimpse. There he would see a sprawling and secular refugee camp: displaced Hindus, Muslims, Sikhs took temporary shelter at 17 York Road, relying on Nehru's hospitality for survival.

The communal carnage which eventually culminated in partition was raging nation-wide. The full fury of primitive brutality was seen as Hindus and Muslims cut each other up in the name of God and country. Yet amid this terrible holocaust and waste of human life there was, almost miraculously, a sense of hope. Freedom, even if it meant dividing the country into two, was at hand. The sun was about to set on the Raj.

Elsewhere in the world there was a semblance of peace. Europe was recovering from the ravages of the Second World War. In America, Truman had taken over the Presidency after Roosevelt's death, while in China Mao tse-Tung was reopening hostilities against his favourite enemy, Chiang-Kai-Shek. In Nuremberg twenty two Nazi leaders, including Goering, were sentenced to death for war crimes, and the first General Assembly of the United Nations met in London with applications for membership from Iceland, Afghanistan, Sweden and Thailand. Frederic March and Olivia de Havilland won Oscars, Mr Yven Petra won Wimbeldon and Herman Hesse won the Nobel Prize for literature.

An anaemic and depleted Indira took off for Mussoorie with her two sons to regain her lost strength. And while she was inhaling the cool mountain air, climactic events were taking place down below.

A truncated India gained freedom, communal riots intensified and a border war with Pakistan was fought—and drawn. Back from Mussoorie, Indira (and her two sons) commuted between husband and father. 'Whenever Feroze got the opportunity he would also come to Delhi.' The arrangement of dual-residence was wholly unsatisfactory—for all concerned. Nehru had a moving daughter-companion, Feroze had a moving wife, and the children had a moving home.

It had been agreed, under the inspiration of Gandhi, that the first native government would set an example by eschewing pomp and show. Simple living was to have been the order of the day. Nehru approved of this war on ostentation, but Mountbatten convinced him that his new status demanded quarters suitable for receiving and entertaining heads of state. Jawaharlal was persuaded, and he moved from the modest 17 York Road to 'Teen Murti', the house of the outgoing British commander-in-chief.

Teen Murti then, as it is today, is a superb example of colonial architecture and colonial life style. The rulers not only ruled but they had to be seen in that capacity. Accordingly, Teen Murti has a north, south, east and west wing; innumerable rooms; mammoth gardens and lawns interspersed with fountains; the distance from the main gate to the actual building is at least one furlong. It is an unfriendly, forbidding, severe mansion which needs a minimum of fifty people to give it any feel of life. As it turned out, no more than four people were to inhabit it. (Today Teen Murti has been converted into the Nehru Museum. His study, bed room and sitting room are maintained as they were on the day of his death. There is also an extensive picture retrospective detailing private and public events. I may be wrong but I don't remember seeing a single photograph of Nehru's son-in-law, Feroze Gandhi.)

Early in 1949 Indira had to make a vital family decision.

With her father installed in his new home and increasingly hosting dinner, tea and breakfast parties she found that she could not spare the time for even her once-a-month trips with the boys to meet Feroze at Lucknow. 'With a heavy heart' she moved in permanently to the Prime Minister's residence, and it was now left to Feroze to do all the running to Delhi if he wished to see his wife and children.

Perhaps another reason why Indira couldn't, or didn't want to, spare the time to visit Lucknow periodically was the increasing competition for the vacant post of 'First Lady of India.' Vijaya Lakshmi coveted the position, so did Krishna, and there were other relatives too who thought they could take advantage of Indira's family preoccupations. Swiftly and surely Mrs Gandhi axed all contenders. The position was hers by right, a fact she asserted bluntly. She was not even prepared to accept helpers. Vijaya Lakshmi and Krishna's family were welcome to stay but on the strict understanding that they were guests. This was Indira's first experience and taste of 'politics', and it must be said that she showed an unerring touch for power jockeying.

For a mother with two children and no, so to speak, husband, Indira had her hands full. As her father's aide she not only had to organize his dishevelled private life but also put up with the vagaries of his invitations. Twenty people would be invited for breakfast and Indira would be the last to be informed. Running the kitchen at Teen Murti alone, as she herself confessed, was a full-time, exhausting and exasperating occupation.

There was, moreover, the attraction of foreign travel. Nehru was constantly being invited overseas and wherever possible he took his daughter: Bandung, China, Europe, America, Russia, England… Mrs Gandhi in the few observations she has made of this period of her life makes out that she found roaming around the world with her father a chore, that she would much rather have stayed back and read bedtime stories to her two boys. I believe she made the sacrifice willingly. Travelling with the Prime Minister and meeting celebrities in five-star comfort must have been a truly exciting experience, and one can't blame her for allowing some parental neglect. Lately, I believe, Mrs Gandhi has expressed some remorse for paying too much attention to her father and too little to her sons at a time of her life when she was not involved in active politics.

Who, in 1950, was going to mind the kids? There is an established tradition in the Nehru family of foreign governesses. Thus both Rajiv and Sanjay, in their formative years, found themselves in the hands of a Danish lady called Anna, who had previously brought up Vijaya Lakshmi's children.

Anna was a governess out of Dickens. Krishna Hutheesingh describes her to perfection: 'She was a strict disciplinarian and ardent believer in cold showers, sunbathing and exercise, and a vegetarian, sometimes subsisting on a diet of raw vegetables and yogurt.' Not, one would think, the ideal companion-teacher for two boys frequently bereft of parental care. Perhaps someone slightly more human and sympathetic than this icy, Nordic governess was required.

Sanjay's early interests in life were completely conventional. Dogs, squirrels, pigeons, ducks, parrots, even tiger cubs consumed his interest. Soon he had his own small, private zoo in Teen Murti. He also liked to 'play trains' for which purpose he engaged his father (whenever available) and grandfather.

The grandfather found the company of his grandsons particularly refreshing. Perhaps the only moments of relief and levity he had in an otherwise taxing, 16-hour day were with Sanjay and Rajiv. And following another Nehru tradition he thoroughly 'spoilt' them. Every whim of the boys was sacrosanct—a luxury which in the case of one of the boys (Sanjay) was to have disastrous consequences.

At four Sanjay was admitted to a kindergarten school, 'Shiv Niketan', in Delhi run by Elizabeth Gauba, a German lady married to an Indian. Mrs Gauba has nothing very illuminating to say about Sanjay. She remembers that he was an 'average boy', that he liked animals more than human beings, that he had lots of self-confidence, that the two brothers were very fond of each other. 'Surprisingly,' she says, 'it was Rajiv who always acted the leader in our plays.' Why surprisingly?

Along with Anna the Dane, one other person looked after the boys—Vimla Sindhi, a robustly proportioned lady who joined the Nehru household as a 'reception officer' in 1950 and left in 1964. During the Emergency, Miss Sindhi was more than forthcoming in the press on Sanjay Gandhi. When I called her up a few months ago she said she 'didn't want to talk' since 'it (Sanjay) was not a pleasant subject.'

Nevertheless, some of Miss Sindhi's Emergency revelations on Sanjay stand repetition. 'He was very fond of mechanics and mending things. He made a little workshop in his room and he was always experimenting. We would ask him to mend little things. He was so neat that if he stuck together a broken object with *Durafix* it looked brand new. But even then he wanted payment—usually a story or a Laurel and Hardy film.'

According to Miss Sindhi, Sanjay was full of pranks. 'Once in Kashmir where we had all gone on holiday I was knitting a sweater for a friend. The sweater was almost complete. One afternoon I woke up after a siesta and could find no trace of it. Finally Mrs Gandhi, after much questioning, got Sanjay to confess that he and Rajiv had undone the sweater and tied the wool from one end of the garden to the other "to see how far Vimi can walk because she is so fat!" I might be biased but I don't think much of that prank.'

The next one is a trifle better: 'During Holi—which was celebrated with much fanfare in the Nehru family—Sanjay asked me to come and see something near a pond. Before I knew what was happening he pushed me into it.'

There was, to be sure, a serious side to the young lad. Vimla Sindhi again: 'Despite the pranks, Sanjay also had a grown-up man's sense of responsibility. Once when we were in Lucknow Mrs Gandhi asked me to bring the boys to Allahabad. I panicked at the idea of having to travel alone with them. "Why are you worried, Vimi?" asked Sanjay. "I will get the tickets and bhai (Rajiv) will take the luggage to the train." They did everything, I just had to relax. We always travelled third class as Mrs Gandhi did not want to spoil the boys.' (This, incidentally, was the kind of stuff being churned out by the massive Sanjay P.R. machinery during the Emergency to convince us that the young lad had all possible leadership qualities.)

The official line, of course, is that 'Indira was a tender mother who gave as much time as possible to the rearing of her two sons, Rajiv and Sanjay. Remembering her own loneliness as a child, she wanted them to have a normal childhood. She supervised their meals, played with them and took them to a film if a suitable one for children was being shown. The boys were secure in their mother's affection.' The official line is, by and large, true. Indira was a tender mother; indeed as far as tenderness was concerned, Jawaharlal, Feroze and Indira were, if anything, over-exuberant—whenever they could spare the time that is.[1] One must remember that these three individuals were furiously busy people who had decided that their respective professional careers would take precedence over their domestic life. Consequently, the boys lapsed into the hands of nannies and reception officers.

Jawaharlal, whenever he could manage a holiday, liked nothing better than going up to Kashmir with his grandsons. Feroze, on his infrequent trips to Delhi, took the boys and his wife for picnics at Okhla. By herself Indira too played the mother's role conscientiously. But attention was mostly sporadic; Sanjay, like all Nehru children, grew up in a vast house, surrounded by servants, smothered with luxury—but essentially alone.

In 1952, Feroze stood for parliamentary elections on a Congress ticket from Raibareilly, and won the seat easily. He moved from Lucknow to Delhi into his father-in-law's house. But not for long.

Feroze grew uneasy in the artificial ceremony proliferating in the P.M.'s house; he couldn't entertain his friends in the manner he was accustomed. (He once asked for coffee at noon in Teen Murti for one of his friends. The servant came back from the kitchen and informed him that coffee time was over.) He didn't like cracks about being 'the nation's son-in-law'. There was, however, one more reason, perhaps paramount. By

1 Sanjay himself rushed to his mother's defence when a 'society lady of means' remarked that because of her public work Indira could not be spending much time with her sons. Said Sanjay to the society lady: 'My mother does lots of important work, yet she plays with me more than you do with your boy.'

now differences—discussed earlier—between the couple had reached such a pitch that any prolonged exposure ensured only strife. Like any married couple having matrimonial difficulties, Feroze and Indira fought—and the kids watched.

A marriage breaking down in front of children is not the best training you can give them in their formative years (Mrs Gandhi is on record: 'We quarelled tremendously'). Wise parent that he was, Feroze moved out to quarters he was allotted as member of parliament. Instead of living with his wife and children he now visited them periodically, usually at breakfast, a ritual family meal at Teen Murti.

Did they visit him? A couple of Mrs Gandhi's apologists insist that, accompanied by her children, Indira regularly but surreptitiously met her husband at his home. 'She would go in the afternoon, quietly.' The question is: why quietly? She was not going off on assignations, she was merely visiting her husband, a visit which should surely have warranted no secrecy. One of Feroze's close Delhi associates told me that he had not once seen either Indira or the children at Feroze's house, neither had he heard anything of secret afternoon visits.

Sanjay by now was ready for formal schooling. And as far as education was concerned, he followed initially at least, in the footsteps of his elder brother.

Besides salubrious climate 'Welham' in Dehradun had other advantages. It was a first-class academic institution, it was close to Delhi, it was a prep for entry into Doon School.

Even today, the persona and reputation of Miss Oliphant looms large in Welham. She was one of those legendary school mistresses whose love for children and education in no way interfered with her ideas of discipline. Both Rajiv and Sanjay passed through her sympathetic hands.

Accompanied by his mother, a seven-year-old Sanjay arrived in Dehradun for enrolment in Welham. It had been quite a task persuading the young lad to go to boarding school. To ease him in, Indira decided to stay on in the circuit house till such time he 'found his feet'.

It took a long time for Sanjay to find his feet. There were physical complications too. His teeth were bad, his eyes hurt, he kept falling sick. A special diet had to be prepared for him.

Miss Oliphant quickly realized that she had a problem child on her hand—a child who would need extra attention for adjustment in a new environment, unlike his brother who had 'settled down in three days'. At morning assembly she told the entire school not to be too inquisitive about the V.I.P. in their midst. 'He is just one more boy—like any of you,' she suggested.

Indira's twice-a-day visits to reassure her son did not help either, although they were designed to do so. After the first week Miss Oliphant recommended that Indira curtail her visits to once-a-day. Alas, there was no improvement. Sanjay was not settling down. He spoke to no one, he played with no one. The only thing he seemed to await each day was his mother's coming.

Miss Oliphant's next tactic was to reduce Indira's once-a-day appearance to once every alternate day, and when even this ploy failed to produce results she requested Indira to leave the boy in school to 'swim with the others'. Indira saw the wisdom of this request and left for Delhi leaving behind a female Parsee secretary, who Miss Oliphant quickly packed off too.

I met Virendra Gaur, one of Sanjay's masters in Welham. 'I don't think Sanjay ever settled down. He was far too attached to his mother, and perhaps spoilt by her. He was not good at studies but neither was he hopeless. Except for swimming he showed no interest in sports. He made few friends and relied mostly on his elder brother, who, incidentally, got on wonderfully with everyone.'

Gaur vividly remembers a picnic. He had taken some of the school boys on a short trek and when they broke for lunch everyone sat around in a circle eating *poori-aloo*. Sanjay refused to join in on the grounds that he was on a special diet. Gaur conceded his error in forgetting to bring special food for Sanjay and suggested he dig into whatever was available. Sanjay refused. Would he at least have the *jalebis*?. No. Fifteen minutes later Sanjay went back to Gaur.

'Sir, I am very hungry.'

'Have you ever eaten this kind of food before?' asked Gaur.

'No.'

'Then why don't you try it?'

Sanjay did. He ate seven *pooris* and confessed, 'Sir, I enjoyed that very much.'

Sanjay seemed to dislike everything connected with school. He did not relish the camaraderie of his fellow students, neither did he enjoy 'swotting', nor did he have any serious extra-curricular interests. But what he disliked most was the annoying anonymity. At Welham he was just one more boy, while in Teen Murti he was the Prime Minister's grandson.

Mr Nehru in particular indulged every Sanjay whim and caprice. Child psychologists, including Benjamin Spock, emphasize the usefulness, indeed necessity, of occasionally saying 'no' to a child. Unfortunately, 'no' was a word Sanjay never heard from his grandfather or from his mother. (I preclude the father because he had very little contact with his son.)

The indulgence could go to ridiculous lengths.

One day Sanjay spotted an electric toy train at the house of one of his friends. When he came home that evening, he demanded that such a train be immediately placed before him. Since the shops had closed by then he was told that enquiries would be made the following morning and, if available, he would get his train. No, he wanted it that very night. Mr Nehru arrived on the scene, and when he heard of his grandson's displeasure he picked up the phone and rang various people in Delhi. The Prime Minister of India and his personal staff spent the next two hours on the telephone hunting the elusive toy! Finally, it was located and just before midnight the train arrived. It was duly presented to Sanjay. Peace prevailed in Teen Murti.

At the age of ten, Sanjay made the expected move—from Welham to Doon School. Mr Nehru was keen that both his grandsons go to Doon, a school he had visited even before his daughter married.

Doon School was an interesting exercise in elitism. There were schools in existence in India where the sons and daughters of the empire builders received the kind of education they would have received 'back home'. Usually a trickling of locals was allowed in for cosmetic purposes rather than for multriracialism. Needless to say that the character of these schools was strongly Christian with emphasis on race loyalty, perpetuation of privilege, clean mind clean body, and the minimum of education.

Doon School was subtly different in its aims and aspirations. The Christian ethic was cleverly disguised by, for example, not insisting on mandatory Bible readings each morning. Instead, secular texts from various scriptures were read to inculcate the required moral values. However, behind this secular veneer the school remained, for all practical purposes, colonial in its outlook. The Raj needed an Indian elite to assist the British administration to run the country—and if this elite was suitably anglicized the job of administration would be that much easier. Consequently, Doon was set up as the kind of institution which would feed the administrative branches of the colonial government with 'the right sort of people'.

The promoters of the school, a motley crowd of 'decorated' Indians and 'emancipated' Britishers, laid down lofty ideals: 'Though slavish imitation is to be avoided, the proposed school will attempt to develop in an atmosphere of Indian culture and environment, many of the best features of English public schools. It will be distinctly Indian in its moral and spiritual outlook, the cultivation of discipline, the building of character, the development of capacity for corporate action, the cultivation of the spirit of chivalry... The school will be residential, as experience has shown that the qualities of manliness and self-reliance are more readily developed in an environment of a residential institution. It will therefore be the aim of the school to foster among its boys a spirit of comradeship uncontaminated by social, communal, religious and provincial prejudices which have impeded the development of a common Indian nationhood.' I have had the privilege and pleasure of knowing many Doscoites and I must say I did not detect in them any of the qualities enumerated in the Doon School charter. (Interestingly, in 1967 when the school invited Mr Morarjee Desai on its Annual Day, Mr Desai had this to say: 'Why do you call me here? You know if I had anything to do with this place I would close it down. Why must we be monkeys and ape the British? When I came here everybody shook my hand, no one said *namaste* to me.')

Feroze, not Indira, escorted Sanjay to Doon School, where both were welcomed by the Headmaster, John Martyn.

I met Mr Martyn some months ago in Mussoorie over tea and cucumber sandwiches. He has an engaging limp, a nicely furrowed face and a fondness for cricket. When the history of Doon is written, John Martyn's name will be pre-eminent. For over three decades, he devoted his life to the school. The open air theatre was built by him, the art classes began under his tenure, mountaineering was his idea, he involved the school in community programmes. With 'geniality and wisdom' he ruled the school. Such was Martyn's devotion to Doon that he found time to marry only after his retirement.

Martyn remembers Sanjay briefly as one of his students. No more. 'I'm afraid I don't remember him,' he told me—an aberration which, surprisingly, does not hold for other students. In the three days I consumed at Doon School talking to masters and such students that had settled in the town, the name Sanjay Gandhi evoked little response or interest. It was uncanny how none of them had any clear memories of the boy. Like Martyn they confirmed he had been a student, but further enquiries drew varieties of vagueness.

A Sanjay contemporary explained to me why it was possible to so easily forget a person no less than the grandson of the Prime Minister of India: 'We didn't bother with titles. I know we should have, but we didn't—perhaps because most of us came from pretty distinguished families ourselves.' Surely he must have some recollections? 'Very few. He was such a colourless character. To stand out in school you have to be either very good or very bad. Sanjay was neither. He was in fact outstandingly mediocre. So he never attracted any attention. Mind you Sanjay was not the only mediocre student. There were a few others like him who just plodded on. To be honest we were somewhat disappointed that the Nehrus had produced such a nondescript human being.'

Some memories, mercifully, are less blank. Sanjay was put into Kashmir House, and his first master, Sahi, immediately noticed some salient characteristics.

Firstly, Sanjay had no aptitude or interest in games. This is by no means a vital disqualification, but in Doon where excellence in sports is cherished even more than excellence in the classroom, it was a serious cause for concern and complaint. Indeed, games were part of the curriculum and participation was compulsory. There were always inter-school, inter-class, inter-house matches in progress, so a boy was constantly being tested. 'He did not even make it into a second house eleven,' said one master with unconcealed contempt.

Sanjay's sporting disqualifications went further: 'Naturally every boy couldn't be a champ, every boy couldn't get into the first eleven. But he didn't even try. I never saw him on the playing field. I don't know how, but he always managed to miss playing. Sometimes he was in hospital, or he had a headache, or he had hurt his foot. Of course he was "shamming", and we knew it.' (I must confess I have complete sympathy with Sanjay for trying to avoid games. There is a kind of vicious public school tyranny which requires boys to shed blood and tears on the playing field, an experience which has emotionally maimed many a sensitive young boy.)

How did he fare in class? No better. Sanjay's attitude to his studies was similar to his attitude to games: he was just not interested. Most masters noticed associated attributes: he never looked you in the eye, he always seemed distant, he very seldom did his homework—and when he did, it was shoddy and careless, he invariably sat in the last row.

If, as a master, you pulled him up for, say, the quality of his school work, the pulling up was received stonily. 'He would stare back at you,' says Kunzru, 'and you always felt you were not getting through. When I reprimanded other boys they might say, "sorry sir", or "I'll do better next time sir". Sanjay said nothing. I could perceive a kind of defiance which seemed to say: "You can do your worst. I won't change". I felt most uncomfortable.'

Gautam Vohra, an assistant editor in the *Times of India*, provides an accurate barometer of Sanjay's scholastic talents as manifested at Doon: 'We had a history teacher called Holdsworth, who had a rather interesting way of grading students. He would ask his class questions and those who answered best moved to the front. I was with Sanjay for one full year in this class and he never went forward. He stayed put in the last row. Even more interesting: he was in no way perturbed by that situation.'

The temptation to conclude that Sanjay was (is) 'stupid' must be resisted. Hari Dang, another of Sanjay's masters, found that although 'his spelling and handwriting were appalling, and although his powers of expression were very poor, he had some good ideas'. At the age of twelve, Sanjay produced a composition for Dang in which he wrote a detailed account of how he would turn the Himalayas into an international playground, with winter games, five star hotels and indoor swimming pools. 'The ideas in the composition were extremely interesting and imaginative, considering the boy was only twelve years old,' says Dang. (No coincidence then that during the Emergency Sanjay contemplated opening Playboy clubs and casinos in the Himalayas.)

Because Sanjay refused to fulfil homework assignments, he was constantly on 'cards', a Doon School form of punishment. Three colours of cards existed: yellow, blue and red. Blue and red cards were given by masters, while the yellow card was a Headmaster's prerogative and denoted the ultimate in school punishment. It is a testimony to Sanjay's consistent mediocrity that he never received the yellow card, instead he was always on the blue and red. John Martyn remembers giving the yellow card to Rajiv but Sanjay 'never got into serious trouble; he was always in minor trouble'.

The card punishment followed an elaborate procedure. A master gave a boy a card for academic or social mischief. The boy took the card to his House Master who, after registering it, initialled the card and returned it to the boy, who in turn returned it to the master. 'If I remember correctly,' says Sandy, a Sanjay contemporary, 'he was always running up and down carrying cards.'

The one thing both masters and students do remember about Sanjay is his 'uncommunicative nature'. The word I heard time and again in reference to Sanjay was 'loner'. The archetypal image of Sanjay in Doon School is of a small boy sitting under a tree far away in thought. 'God knows what he was thinking, what made him so desperately sad.'

Sanjay's loneliness was made even more crushing by his inability to make friends. Since he spoke to no one, no one spoke to him. 'I tried to talk to him, I really did. I suppose I was interested in finding out what a Nehru grandson would be like. He snubbed me straight away. After that I ignored him. I am sure he treated other offers of friendship in the same way,' says Pawan, a Doon school student who runs a petrol station in Dehradun today.

Sandy has a different explanation for Sanjay's loneliness: 'Who wanted to make friends with him? He was such a dull and boring character. Whenever you saw him he looked miserable and unhappy. Who would want to mix with such a duffer?'

There has been speculation that Sanjay was on the receiving end of massive 'ragging' which is supposed to account for his sullen behavior. Certainly Sanjay was the kind of 'boy seniors love to rag; but in Doon there is no tradition of methodical and severe ragging, what exists is "fagging"'. So Mr Gandhi's unhappy school life cannot be attributed to his head being flushed in a filthy toilet.

Sanjay's passion for birds persisted. Once when he caught a sparrow in his mosquito net he was delighted. Mrs Sahi, the House Matron, remembers: 'He was really proud of his captive bird. I have never seen him look happier.' Alas, one of Sanjay's roommates freed the bird in his absence, and when he returned he was furious, foaming at the mouth. Sanjay looked around for reprisals. He saw the boy's new tennis racket, a Dunlop 'Maxply'. Sanjay picked up the racket and smashed it to smithereens. (When I recount this tale to my friends, they immediately see a parallel between Sanjay's desire to cage the bird and his desire 'to cage the nation'. I see no such parallel; Sanjay merely wanted to capture a bird—something most of us have done or wanted to do in our youth.)

Both Jawaharlal and Indira behaved, in the words of John Martyn, as 'very normal parents. They wanted the boys to have no special privileges. I don't think they came very often. Even when they did they came and went without fuss.'

In the case of mother and grandfather the boys had some kind of forewarning. The routine was to pick them up and take them to the only restaurant in town, 'Kwality'. Sanjay was particularly partial to Kwality toffees (a partiality he retains till today) which they bought him in huge quantities.

Rajiv and Sanjay knew by now that they had estranged parents. A fact which was made poignantly clear to them when on one particular day they had a visit from the mother in the morning and the father in the evening. The poignancy was heightened when both parents took the boys to the same restaurant—Kwality—and stayed in adjoining rooms in the circuit house.

In a sea of loneliness and anonymity, Sanjay turned to the nurse in the school hospital. He was constantly approaching her on the pretext of having a cold or an upset stomach or a headache. Frequently the nurse found that there was nothing medically wrong with him, but she understood his problem and gave him the solace he needed. 'He wanted a bit of extra attention and since he was not getting it from the boys or the masters, he turned to the nurse,' says Kunzru.

The attention he found lacking in school he found in ample measure at Teen Murti. During mid-term breaks, when most boys preferred to go on trekking or fishing or mountain climbing expeditions, Sanjay preferred to go home. And it was during one of these breaks that Sanjay told Marie Seton: 'I hate school. I don't want to go back.'

Hari Deo Bhatt, the Hindi teacher at Doon, was fortunate to get Sanjay away during one mid-term break, and he was witness to a remarkable display of bravado.

Sanjay, Rajiv, Mr and Mrs Bhatt were going downstream on a school-built raft. Although the water was not very deep, there was a strong current. Suddenly, the raft split into two. Precariously perched on one side were Sanjay and Mr Bhatt, while on the other Rajiv and Mrs Bhatt clutched tightly. All the passengers, especially Bhatt, were understandably nervous, except young Sanjay who jumped up and down on his side of the raft shouting: 'What fun.'

Hari Deo Bhatt was the recipient of a rare privilege. He was asked to take Rajiv, Sanjay and a few other boys to Delhi. All the boys stayed in Teen Murti where Mr Nehru hosted a special dinner in their honour.

When Feroze heard that his sons were in town he sent a message to Bhatt asking him to bring the boys to Parliament House. 'We went,' Bhatt told me, 'into the visitors' gallery where Sanjay saw his father make a stirring speech. After some time Feroze came out to the visitors gallery. As soon as he saw his sons he rushed towards them and embraced them simultaneously—one under each arm. I cannot describe the scene, it was like a meeting of long lost souls.'

Feroze did manage to occasionally snatch his sons away from Teen Murti. He would take them home, show them his garden, his hunting trophies, his fishing tackle. He also gave them what he thought were necessary lessons—like sawing wood. Asked by a friend why he was giving his boys such menial training, Feroze said: 'My sons have a very rich mother but a very poor father. I am making sure they don't starve.'

After a year in Doon, Sanjay did make a couple of friends. And the people he befriended were, by and large, like him: rich, spoilt, academically dim, uninterested in sports. There was Kamal Nath from Calcutta, a voluble, loud lad who liked 'to throw his money around' and 'who failed two years in a row'. There was 'Scampi' of Jind, plus one of the Kapoorthalas, and other assorted nobility. Today, one is an alcoholic, another has become a hermit while Kamal Nath is under enquiry for Emergency excesses.

Together they formed some sort of group. Sanjay's role was not that of leader (a position reserved for Kamal Nath): he played, as usual, a 'quiet behind-the-scenes' role, planning and master-minding group activities.

Under the guidance of Kamal Nath there was some smoking and drinking done and occasionally 'bounds' were broken—activities which most 'normal' school boys get up to.

Individually, Sanjay had the reputation of being 'a bit of a kleptomaniac'. One Doon School boy told me that when Sanjay entered a room everyone clutched on to his belongings. He also had a weakness for hubcaps from cars as he had for the Mercedes emblem (removed from vehicles coming into the school). Sanjay boasted a fair collection of these, and on one occasion when they were discovered in his room 'the matter was quickly hushed up.'

Sanjay tried his hand at some petty forgery, too. The 'tuck shop' in Doon School worked, instead of cash, on a system of signing. Sanjay was fairly famous for forging other boys' names on his chits; he also forged his House Master's signature on his 'cards'. When I asked one of the masters about these counterfeit activities he said: 'He may have, but I don't recollect any complaint. Most boys get up to these kind of things. It's quite normal.'

Then there was Sanjay's well-renowned love for motor cars. On feast nights when parents would drive in to Dehradun to dine with their sons, Sanjay and his mates would prowl around looking for unlocked cars, preferably with the ignition keys dangling. Such cars were whisked away for short, fast drives and brought back before they were missed. Although both masters and students corroborate Sanjay's car pinching penchant, there is no record in Doon of him being caught in the act.

Perhaps the most startling private Sanjay revelation to emerge from Doon concerns his homosexuality. Startling because subsequently in life Sanjay has provided abundant proof of his heterosexuality. 'It was common knowledge in Kashmir House that he was a homosexual,' says Sandy. And so do many others. Superficially, of course, Sanjay fits the homosexual pattern only too neatly: shy, introverted, lonely, unsuccessful... However, I suspect, Sanjay's interest in men was voyeuristic, part of a public school tradition, a phase which many a boy educated in an Anglo-Indian school passes through without any permanent sexual scars. Indeed, and I echo a public school philosophy, it may have been a salutary experience.

An exciting person Sanjay met at this period of his life was Yuri Gagarin, the first man in space. Gagarin, a state guest, was invited to a private dinner at Teen Murti at which Sanjay was present. While everyone was busy throwing questions at Gagarin about his experiences in space, Sanjay listened quietly as the Russian explained the rigorous training and complicated machinery he had to master before embarking on his flight. After the dinner Sanjay told his mother: 'What's so great about Gagarin? After all, he was only an instrument.'

To every student/master I met, I posed one standard question: 'Did Sanjay display any signs of callousness or cruelty, qualities he allegedly displayed during the Emergency?' The majority replied in the negative. One Sanjay contemporary, and by no means an admirer, went as far as to say: 'I was really surprised to read all the things he is supposed to have done. In school he was the kind of guy who wouldn't hurt a fly.'

Indira and Feroze, meanwhile, made periodic attempts to repair their marriage. And they tried to build the reconciliation around the kids, the well-tested adhesive for crumbling marriages. G. M. Sadiq of Kashmir provided the necessary backdrop: a duck shoot 100 miles from Srinagar. Indira, Feroze, Rajiv, Sanjay spent a couple of happy and carefree days in the mountains. But reconciliation was short lived. The Indira-Feroze marriage, it became clear, could not be patched up with duck shoots or emotional cries of 'what will happen to the children'.

In Doon School it was customary at the end of each term for the House Master to send a kind of progress report to the parent detailing general observations on the student's behaviour and disposition. This was beyond the official mark sheet which carried results obtained in specific subjects.

'Joe' Joshi was Sanjay's House Master in his third year. And like most other masters he was greatly puzzled by the boy. There was obviously nothing wrong with him; he was not dumb or retarded, yet he refused to enter into the spirit of school life— both in and out of the classroom. Joshi checked with other masters who also expressed their inability 'to get anything out of the boy'. Of course he passed each year—but just. However, what worried Joshi most was the unanimous opinion of staff members that they were making 'no contact' with Sanjay. 'He seems to resent us', wrote one master to Joshi.

A bewildered Joshi communicated his and other staff members' problems with Sanjay to Mrs Gandhi. Could she help?

Mrs Gandhi's reply surprised the school, especially the Headmaster, John Martyn. In response to Joshi's request for help she wrote back saying she was removing her son from school. 'You must understand, we did not ask Mrs Gandhi to take the boy away,' says Martyn, 'it was entirely her decision. We would have been quite happy to keep him on.' I asked Kunzru how the reports in the press about Sanjay being 'expelled' from Doon emanated. 'I don't know. As far as we are concerned Sanjay was not expelled, it was Mrs Gandhi who called him back to Delhi.'

Two reasons are forwarded for Mrs Gandhi's abrupt termination of Sanjay's studies in Doon. Firstly, Sanjay had been clamouring to come home anyway. He had told his mother repeatedly that he was miserably unhappy in school and would much rather study as a day-scholar in Delhi.

Secondly, with Rajiv away in England, Teen Murti was devoid of the edifying laughter of children. Mr Nehru in particular missed both his grandsons greatly and wanted one at least by his side. Interestingly, when he was asked why Sanjay had been reclaimed from Doon, Nehru said: 'He was not doing well in his studies. If he is nearer home he might improve.' I don't think that explanation is the whole truth. Mr Nehru was not so much concerned about Sanjay's education as he was about company for himself.

All the masters, including John Martyn, are convinced that Indira and Jawaharlal made a terrible mistake by withdrawing Sanjay before time. 'Some boys are late developers,' says Martyn, 'they take time to blossom out. I have known many boys who were like Sanjay initially but later improved tremendously. If Sanjay had stayed on, who knows—he may have been a different person.'

It was while Sanjay and Rajiv were in Doon School that they heard the news of their father's death.

Feroze had his first heart attack in 1958, from which he seemed to have recovered quite nicely. 'He was back in full spirits, laughing and joking as before.' On 7 September 1960 he had his second attack from which he did not recover.

Feroze Gandhi's death was characteristic of the man. He woke up on the morning of September 7 with a pain in his chest. Instead of calling a doctor or going to the hospital he went, as usual, to the House where he met his journalist friend, Inder Malhotra. Inder couldn't help noticing his friend's physical condition. Feroze laughed off the pain but later agreed to go to the hospital, refusing Inder's offer to drive him there. Alone, he drove to Willingdon Hospital, and collapsed while checking in.

Indira was attending a women's convention in Kerala from where she returned in haste to be at her husband's bedside. The next morning at 7.45 he had a coughing spell. 'Indira immediately took his head in her hands, but before she could realize what had happened, Feroze's countenance clouded over'.

Rajiv lit the funeral pyre, while Mr Nehru was amazed at the number of mourners his son-in-law had attracted. 'I never knew he was so popular,' he remarked. In a letter to a friend, Mrs Gandhi broke down: 'I am feeling so utterly desolate and miserable. You know how much Feroze and I disagreed and quarelled over the years and yet, instead of separating and slackening the bond of friendship, we were closer than before... The boys are of an age when they need a father more than a mother. I feel lost and empty and dead.'

So Feroze Gandhi died at the age of 48. An unhappy man, I think, for most of his life, torn between his own appetites and ambitions and his fundamentally good nature.

As his father's body lay cold in Teen Murti, Sanjay stood 'like a tree that had been struck by lightning'. Father and son had been especially close, and Feroze was probably marginally fonder of his younger son, presumably because they both 'liked doing things with their hands'. Currently, it is Rajiv who cherishes the memory of his father more fondly, while Sanjay is fairly matter-of-fact. Asked in 1976 whether he was close to his father, Sanjay replied cryptically: 'Yes—like any son is to his father.' (Rajiv proudly displays in his room mementos of his late father—the ash tray, the watch, the pipe, the gun and many photographs. 'He gets very emotional when he talks about his father, and very angry when he hears any criticism of him,' says a Rajiv friend.)

From Doon, Sanjay shifted to St. Columbus, Delhi from where he is supposed to have done his I.S.C. and obtained '21 points'. When I tried to confirm with St. Columbus they were most reluctant to part with any information except the fact that Sanjay had been a student. Critics maintain that while Sanjay may have been admitted in St. Columbus he did not in fact pass any exams. Actually, he did., However, Maneka's claim that her husband holds a 'diploma in mechanical engineering' is pure fantasy. The sum total of Sanjay's educational qualifications is an I.S.C. from St. Columbus in Delhi.

WHAT SANJAY ENJOYED AS a day-scholar in St. Columbus, Delhi, was the absence of boarding school discipline. There were no 'lights out' at Teen Murti, no 'bounds', no record of entry or exit. Sanjay could go as he pleased, he could come as he pleased.

The central metaphor in Sanjay's indiscipline was, naturally, the motor car. In the company of Adil Sharyar (Mohammed Yunus's, son) Sanjay exhibited a range of interests—all, however, connected with motor vehicles.

He purchased an 'ancient derelict car' at a throwaway price, and then went scouring the city for spare parts. Soon he had some sort of moving machine ready in which he and Adil zipped around town. Recalls Adil: 'Sanjay drove very recklessly. He was always driving into ditches... He drove through ploughed fields and rocky hillsides.'

But Sanjay was not the kind of person to be satisfied with a derelict car. He was continually experimenting with Jeeps, Land Rovers, Fiats, Ambassadors... Occasionally, the experimenting was tinged with danger: 'One day he came in a second hand Land Rover and asked me to accompany him as he wanted to test the brakes. He took the car to a steep hillock near Vasant Vihar and just let it come down. Luckily the brakes worked or I wouldn't be here today' says Adil.

Whether he was going to Corbett Park or on holidays or for picnics, the car was indispensible. Destinations were fixed but not always adhered to. A friend recounts: 'He asked me if I would like to go to Simla for a holiday. When I agreed, he just jumped into the car, picked up some more friends and we took off. Halfway on our journey he asked me if I would like to go instead to Srinagar. The matter was put to vote: the majority was for Srinagar. So off we went to Srinagar.'

Indira was, understandably, distressed at the recklessness of her son. Frequently she was ignorant of his whereabouts and when she asked him he was not always prepared to tell.

Moreover, most of his interests seemed to be nocturnal, which was a further cause for motherly concern. Mrs Gandhi's friends had warned her earlier that, without the constraints of boarding school, her son might fall into bad company, and worse, indulge his wayward passion for cars, a premonition which seemed to be turning true on both counts.

Indira's fears were further stoked in early '64. Almost every day she read in the papers of a new Delhi phenomenon: car thefts. *The Times of India* in May that year reported: 'Though the police will not admit it officially, they suspect a gang of teenagers, who steal cars for joy-rides and abandon them later.' The paper went on to insinuate that college boys of 'influential people' were involved in these thefts.

The 'big' theft took place on May 16. Late at night, an almost 'brand new Fiat' belonging to an Army officer was lifted from Nizamuddin East, driven to a petrol station (20 litres of petrol were filled without payment) and later discarded near Palam airport. When the police recovered the vehicle the next morning they discovered inside a girl's underwear, a rope, an iron rod, a can of petrol and a few empty bottles of liquor.

More complications. That very night a motorcycle had been stolen and smashed. The driver was lying unconscious in a nursing home. He was identified as Adil Sharyar, Sanjay's 'bosom buddy'.

The role of the police was curious, to say the least. On the morning of May 17 they informed the Army officer that his car had been located. Would he call at Moti Bagh police station to identify it. The owner, of course, was grateful for the safe recovery of his car; he was, however, keen to discover the names and addresses of the culprits. When, after a month, he made enquiries, he was greeted with evasions and the usual 'investigations are proceeding' routine. One police officer did offer a hint: 'Some big, very big people's sons are involved in it.' Dosu Karaka, the late editor of *Current,* did not believe in insinuations or hints. In a front page story he named Sanjay as one of the key people in the car theft and he challenged Mrs Gandhi to clear her son's name. Although other papers did not make the charge so openly, they did imply that one of the 'influential people's sons' was Sanjay Gandhi.

While speculations and charges were raging in the press, Indira Gandhi maintained total silence. 'Sanjay was very sore with his mother for not denying the charge. Everyone in Teen Murti knew that on May 16 he was hitchhiking in Kashmir and was not in Delhi. He told me himself later on in England that he tried his best to persuade his mother to make a public statement,' Marie Seton told me. I asked Marie why Mrs Gandhi had so stubbornly refused to deny the charge. 'I asked her the same question, and she told me that it would make no difference. "You know what the Indian press is like" she said. Personally, I believe Indira should have made a statement.'

Was Sanjay in Kashmir on the crucial date? Or was he (and a friend) 'packed off to Srinagar by an early morning flight on May 17 and they had turned up later that evening at the house of a Muslim lady teacher who was to be their host at Srinagar. They had taken care to arrive at the lady's house looking like real hitchhikers with mud splattered all over their trousers and shoes.'

The hitchhiking in Kashmir story is corroborated by many, admittedly partisan, sources, which makes Mrs Gandhi's silence on the subject all the more baffling. However, even if one pronounces Sanjay innocent of this particular 'prank', there is no denying he was involved in other car thefts around the same time. Mrs Gandhi's reluctance to jump to her son's defence was based on fears of raking up other, dormant car thefts in which she knew her son had participated. In the circumstances, I think, she made the right decision hoping that the storm would blow over—a calculation which held good for 13 years.

A week after Sanjay's alleged car theft, Mr Nehru died of a stroke—with both his grandsons absent. Rajiv was away at Cambridge (he arrived a day later) while Sanjay was still hitchhiking in Kashmir. A special plane, courtesy G. M. Sadiq, brought him back to the capital in time to light the funeral pyre. Marie Seton was there: 'It was incredible, this boy of 17 dressed in white, surrounded by these masses of people howling and wailing and shouting, stood erect, cool as a cucumber. I don't think I saw a tear on his face. He seemed totally unaffected by what was going on around him.'

Mr Khushwant Singh, during the Emergency, gently probed Sanjay on his relationship with his grandfather.

Q: Were you close to him?

A: As close as other people are to their grandfathers.

Q: Did he influence your thinking in any way?

A: I cannot recall any specific way in which he influenced me.

Nehru doted on Sanjay as if the latter was his own son. But I am not sure if the affection and love were reciprocated equally. Both Sanjay and Rajiv, I suspect, in the later stages of their life counted their grandfather among the major factors in the break-up of their family life, a conclusion not likely to engender great feelings of love and affection.

Probably one reason why the finger of suspicion fell so readily on Sanjay in the car theft case was the discovery of a girl's underwear inside the vehicle. In Delhi, Mr Gandhi's preference for motor cars was nearly as well publicized as his preference for pretty girls. To be fair, in Sanjay's list of priorities the car came first, with women a close second.

While researching this book I heard some fantastic tales—most of them unprintable—detailing Sanjay's bizarre sexual habits. I am pretty certain that they are grossly exaggerated, if not entirely fiction. Indeed, between 'he wanted a new woman every night' and 'the only woman he has known in his life is Maneka' the truth is hard to locate.

A few truths are indisputable. Like most normal, growing boys Sanjay showed a 'healthy' interest in sex and the opposite sex, an interest traceable from Sanjay's Doon School days through his fondness for telling and listening to 'dirty jokes'. He was not particularly moral or righteous either: if he fancied a girl— and he fancied most girls—he pursued her.

What was shattering for him was a conclusion he was forced to reach as he grew from adolescence to manhood: women were not attracted to him. And for good reason. He was no scintillating conversationalist, he was akward and shy, he possessed no sense of humour, he had no sporting or scholastic talents, he was no millionaire, he was, to put it charitably, 'OK to look at'. He seemed to have none of the qualities women look for in their men.

Save one. He had connections, albeit gratuitous, with power. (And we all know that the most potent aphrodisiac in the world, as Mr Henry Kissinger proved, is power.) As Sanjay Gandhi, women ignored him; as the Prime Minister's son, they clustered around him. Some of these ladies had political ambitions, others were encouraged by their parents, 'to get friendly' in the hope of 'roping him into marriage', others merely relished the thrill of flirting in the corridors of power.

Nevertheless, Sanjay reaped a meagre harvest from these categories. His biggest catch came from elsewhere. 'If you were a businessman—like Kuldip Narang—and you wanted something done by him or through him, the easiest way to achieve your purpose was to exploit his weakness for women. Even if the businessman required no immediate favours, he would keep him happy for possible future favours by providing the necessary bait', says a middle man who claims 'he was there'.

The knowledge that women came to him only through 'the mother connection' must have come as a tremendous blow to Sanjay's male vanity. But he seemed to have quickly reconciled himself to that fact and subsequently showed no compunctions in using nepotism to 'get his girls'.

Among Sanjay's womanizing stories to surface the most sensational is that of the Jagotta[2] brothers. Late one night, the brothers attempted to meet Sanjay to discuss their sister. Apparently he had got the girl into 'trouble' and the brothers demanded he do the 'honourable' thing. When security at Mrs Gandhi's house checked about letting in the two men, Sanjay refused, repeating that they were to be allowed in under no circumstances. Some altercation took place at the gate. The brothers finally backed their car, but instead of turning around they crashed into 1, Safdarjung. The gate broke and the car proceeded inside. It was, however, apprehended quickly and the brothers were arrested and jailed for breaching security.

---

2 The Sanjay camp says that the brothers were trying to plant the girl in the P.M.'s household.

The story was briefly reported in the press and then quickly hushed up.

On 29 July 1974 there was a small announcement in the press concerning Sanjay's engagement to one Maneka Anand. 18-year-old Maneka, the announcement revealed, was taking a course in German at the Jawaharlal Nehru University and also working as a journalist for a weekly called 'Delhi Dateline'. Previously she had studied political science at Lady Shri Ram College.

Beginning in 1974 Miss Anand was plastered all over Delhi. 'A lanky, vivacious college beauty queen' (crowned 'Miss Lady Sri Ram College' in '73), she had recently taken to modelling with great success. Dressed scantily in a towel, she was seen on billboards and press ads promoting Delhi Cloth Mills. On July 28, the advertising agency handling the D.C.M. account got a call from Mrs Anand who demanded all pictures and transparencies of her daughter back. Overnight, all the sexy hoardings with Maneka were removed while the press campaign was hastily scrapped. Maneka's promising modelling career came to an abrupt end.

Although one hears of various irregular reasons for the Sanjay-Maneka match, there is a fairly straightforward explanation: Cupid had struck Sanjay. Mrs Usha Bhagat, who was then working in the Prime Minister's house, wrote to a friend: 'He has fallen head over heels in love'.

The courtship was entirely correct and conventional. Sanjay asked the late Col Anand for his daughter's hand, and while the latter had no objection, he suggested that Sanjay consult his mother. Mrs Gandhi was relieved to hear that her son was settling down. However, she was 'not sure if Maneka was the right girl for Sanjay'. Indira had a long, serious chat with Maneka in which she emphasized two points.

Firstly, her son was 'difficult' to live with. Secondly, and this worried Indira most, he was almost ten years her senior. Maneka's replies were brief: she was aware about his being difficult and she understood the problems posed by the age difference. Love, however, would conquer all.

The marriage ceremony on 29 September 1974 was surprisingly simple. Mr Mohammed Yunus's house was chosen as the venue and besides close family members (Feroze's two sisters were present) there were no more than thirty guests. The marriage was solemnized under the Civil Marriages Act 'by the Registrar of Civil Marriages, Navin Chawla'. Mrs Anand, Mrs Gandhi and Mr Yunus signed as witnesses.

Dressed in a white khadi sherwani and pyjama, Sanjay slipped on the wedding ring to a Maneka clad in a khadi saree. 'The couple exchanged *Jawala* and offered sweets to each other. Rose petals and flowers were showered on the couple by family and friends.'

Such was Mrs Gandhi's insistence on secrecy that she refused permission to both Delhi TV and Films Division to be present for the wedding. A lone photographer, however, did sneak in and supplied the press with 'simple photographs'. The *Illustrated Weekly* did not fail to note the outstanding feature of the wedding: 'Maneka is a Sikh, Sanjay's mother is a Hindu, his father was a Parsee and they were married in the house of a Muslim—true to our secular ideals'. Next morning, instead of flying off for a honeymoon, Maneka went to her German classes while Sanjay went to his car factory.

The Sanjay-Maneka marriage has worn reasonably well. In fact, if Sanjay appears calm and composed while 'hounded like a rat' some credit could go to his wife. Initially, it is true that Maneka's influence in the Gandhi household was slight.

Sonia was the senior daughter-in-law and she performed in 1, Safdarjung precisely the duties Mrs Gandhi performed at Teen Murti. Sonia was (is) the queen of the kitchen, she purchased sarees for her mother-in-law and when someone like Andre Malraux came for dinner, she fixed the guest list. It is more than likely that in those days young Maneka felt left out. Currently, Maneka has gained ground. In the pages of *Surya*, the house magazine of 12 Willingdon Crescent, she conducts every month a spirited and sometimes vicious defence of her husband and her mother-in-law. 'No one gave the marriage more than a year,' says a family friend, 'and if Mrs Gandhi had won the elections and Sanjay had become king, they would certainly have split up. In the changed circumstances, however, it is Sanjay who needs his wife.'

Maruti: Son of the Wind God

'LET'S GO FOR A walk,' suggested Sanjay to Marie Seton.[1] The year was 1960. Marie was a house guest of the Nehrus and Sanjay was on vacation from his school in Dehradun.

They strolled into the expansive and blooming gardens of Teen Murti and walked in silence. Marie remembers a certain bewilderment. Why had he asked her for a stroll? Was he in some trouble? Did he have something on his mind? She decided she wasn't going to ask. They kept walking. The silence persisted. Then, suddenly, Sanjay stopped, looked Marie straight in the face and said, 'When I grow up, I am going to make cars.'

---

1 An old and devoted friend of India and the Nehrus. Author of books on subjects as varied as Eisenstein, Paul Robeson and Jawaharlal Nehru.

The motor car had always fascinated Sanjay. In his grandfather's house he would gape wide-eyed as this mechanical contraption whisked in and out. Apparently, all that was required was the turning of a key, and zoom ... Sanjay was determined to explore the mysteries behind this seemingly simple yet power-invested act.

Even as a child, Sanjay's favourite toys had been those with buttons and keys, and those which moved. On his sixth birthday Panditji presented Sanjay with a pedal car, and this instantly became the boy's proudest possession. On the lawns of Teen Murti, grandfather would push the car and the grandson would take off with what he thought was great speed.

It is more than possible that Sanjay's car curiosity came via his genes. Feroze had his own small black Morris which he kept spotlessly black. Among the things he enjoyed most was polishing his car and uncovering its bonnet. A tinkerer by temperament, he always managed to find a spark plug which needed cleaning, a screw which needed tightening, a bolt which needed oiling. Although father and son didn't spend much time together, Sanjay had seen Feroze at work on his car. Feroze had tried to explain to his son how a car worked and what part the different components played in its running. The son was too young to understand, but his interest was kindled.

Marie isn't certain whether she was the first to hear of Sanjay's adult ambitions. However, by the time he left Doon School he had told both his mother and grandfather what he had told Marie in the gardens of Teen Murti.

Nehru was delighted with his grandson's choice of career. He had frequently expressed his admiration for Sanjay's instinctive skill in all things electrical. 'Sanjay knows more about electricity than all of us put together,' Nehru informed a gathering of friends. 'He is' he added rashly, 'going to be a great engineer one day.'

Before one could make cars, however, one needed to get the requisite educational training. Indira and Nehru were keen that Sanjay take a degree in mechanical engineering before he got down to designing and manufacturing cars.

Sanjay wasn't so keen. He was against going to 'one more college.' According to him, the best way of learning how to make a car was to work in a car factory. Swayed by their knowledge of Sanjay's mediocre scholastic record, Indira and Nehru agreed to drop the mechanical engineering idea.

If Sanjay was going to learn his trade in a car factory, it had to be the best. Dr Dharam Teja,[2] a dubious family friend, organized an apprenticeship at the Rolls-Royce plant in Crewe, England. The three-year apprenticeship required a student to work on the shop floor, moving from department to department. To supplement practical training, apprentices enrolled in the local technical college for evening classes.

Sanjay arrived in Crewe in September 1964. He moved into a company-owned hostel for management trainee apprentices who had come from outside the immediate locality of Crewe. In Sanjay's batch there were 20 such apprentices, each on a salary of £9 per week.

Not a great deal is known about the life and times of Sanjay Gandhi in Crewe. Characteristically, he didn't make many friends, preferring his own company to others. Occasionally,

---

2 A shipping tycoon who used his Nehru connection to build a private fortune. Arrested in 1966 and sentenced to three years' imprisonment.

he would go over to Marie Seton's flat in London. Rajiv, studying in Cambridge, would also be invited and the two brothers would spend time together.

Actually, Rajiv didn't have much time to spare. He had a lady friend, an Italian girl called Sonia, whom he had met in Cambridge. (Marie had given Rajiv a key of her flat so that he and Sonia could come and go as they pleased.) Moreover, Rajiv had made numerous new friends at the university and seemed to have a very full and hectic social life.

Sanjay's social life was a little less hectic. Marie was bothered because she never saw Sanjay with a girl.

'Sanjay, how would you like to meet some girls? I could introduce you to some,' offered Miss Seton.

'Certainly not,' was Sanjay's terse reply.

Sanjay was not averse to feminine company. I suspect he just didn't relish the idea of 'help.' Certainly David Trevannion and Freddie Whitelaw[3] noticed no misogynist-teetotaler tendencies. David: 'I don't think he drank or had any more to do with women than the rest of us. Of course we did drink and we went to parties and he used to come along. As far as women go there were a lot worse.' Freddie: 'We all drank a fair amount and went out with girls, and it would have been strange if he didn't show any interest in women.' Trevannion remembers another Sanjay interest: 'He was very interested in politics. He would talk about politics all the time. But always Indian politics. He was very scathing about British politics.'

What did David think of him as a person? 'If you asked me now whether I liked him, I would say no, but he was certainly an interesting person to know. The reason I didn't like him was

---

3 Two of Sanjay's British apprentice contemporaries at Crewe.

his inflexibility. He kept to his point of view and once he'd made up his mind about anything you could never get him to alter his opinion. He argued with other apprentices a lot.'

As expected, Sanjay got into trouble. In December 1966 he was arrested for driving without a valid licence, a fairly serious offence in England. Sanjay pleaded guilty by letter, thus avoiding appearance in court, and paid a fine of Rs. 100. The Indian papers made much of this prank. David Trevannion recalls: 'He used to drive fast cars and I remember he had a Jaguar 120. Part of the trouble with his driving was that I don't think he ever managed to get an English driving licence. I can't remember any specific incidents but I recall he didn't like stopping at red lights. Also, when he had crashed a car or something, he used to think that was very funny.'

On another occasion, 'Returning from London one night in a car which he had souped up to "do a ton" up the motorway, he went out of control and rolled over twice. He escaped but the High Commission had some embarassment in hushing up complaints about the daredevil driver.'

Sanjay had completed two out of his three years at Rolls-Royce when he announced he was leaving. 'I have learned everything there is to learn. I would be wasting my time if I stayed on any longer,' he told a friend. Subsequently, Sanjay has stuck to this explanation as his reason for leaving a prized apprenticeship unfinished.[4]

The 'learned everything' explanation doesn't stand up to examination; in fact it is ludicrous. One could believe it of someone who was a brilliant student and was thus capable of mastering a three-year course in two. The three-year Rolls-

---

4 He now says: 'I wasn't learning fast enough.'

Royce apprenticeship is only a generalized training programme designed to prepare students for a more comprehensive course. If Sanjay had been serious about 'learning' he would not only have completed his full term but stayed on a year or so for specialization. No, the reasons for Sanjay leaving lie elsewhere, indeed we have heard them before.

What happened to Sanjay at Rolls-Royce was what happend to Sanjay in Doon School. He was sullen, aloof, wilful and not overly interested in the curriculum. A Rolls-Royce apprenticeship, among the best of its kind in the world, is closely monitored and supervised by a team of engineers. All of them found this particular apprentice difficult, uncooperative and prone to doing things his own way. Thus, when he announced he was leaving, they didn't try to stop him.

Whitelaw says he was surprised at Sanjay's leaving, 'But there have been other people through the same scheme—people like the son of David Brown, the fellow who owned Aston Martin—who left in between. The company knows that people like Sanjay Gandhi, who come in on a great favour, aren't going to last out. So in a way the investment is wasted. These people are inclined to leave at short notice.'

The last word is best left to the P.R.O. of the Rolls-Royce factory at Crewe: 'All he (Sanjay) was interested in was booze and women.'

DRIVING AROUND SOUTH DELHI, Rajiv heard a bang from under his car. He stopped, got out and discovered his Ambassador had burst a tyre. Fortunately, he spied a puncture shop opposite, which, as it turned out, was owned by Arjun Das.

Arjun Das repaired the puncture. He also made an impression on Rajiv. Despite his physical disabilities, 'short, squat, dark,.... clownish, something of a *pahelwan*', Arjun Das had an unmistakeable appeal, a no-nonsense, frontal approach to problems, plus an amazingly wide knowledge of automobiles gleaned not from text books but from actual mechanic experience. Rajiv introduced Sanjay to Arjun Das, and Sanjay was even more impressed. Of course, they had one consuming interest in common: cars.

Arjun Das was a gold-mine of rare and secret information. He knew all the Delhi junkyards and workshops and he also knew the 'chor bazaars'. Together Sanjay and Arjun Das plundered these markets for spare parts. They hired a shed in Gulabi Bagh and set to work on what was later to be known as 'Maruti'—the son of the wind god.

From the middle of 1967, Sanjay worked like a demon in his workshop. He would leave at 8 in the morning and return late at night—and then get straight down to paperwork. Indira was concerned at the excessive devotion her son was showing to his work. She became even more worried when Sanjay got badly burnt as a result of an explosion in his workshop.

One of Sanjay's friends describes the locale and the interior of the workshop. '...Gulabi Bagh was then a filthy truck shop surrounded by garbage dumps and overflowing sewers. The workshop itself was crowded with bits and pieces of twisted metal, rusting parts, and a giant-sized hand-operated press on which wheel hubs were formed, one hole at a time. Sanjay was not discouraged and immediately set about with the first Maruti prototype on a makeshift roof structure right above the 100-square-foot-odd space, with various equipment resting precariously all around.'

Not so slowly, Arjun Das gained the respect and confidence of Mrs Gandhi. More than a versatile mechanic, he was the protector of her son whose propensity for getting into fights and altercations was well known. Soon Arjun Das was moving in and out of 1, Safdarjung with the ease of a family member. If he happened to be around at meal times, he automatically stayed on. Such was Arjun Das's relationship with the Prime Minister that he could confidently claim: 'I am the third son of Mrs Gandhi'—a sentiment Indira fully reciprocated when in 1972 she campaigned for him in the municipal elections and declared 'I don't have two sons, I have three...'

In all the literature written after the Emergency, Arjun Das emerges painted with one uniform black brush. His modest family background, his inability to speak English, his lack of sophistication, his 'rough hands' seem to have caused great aesthetic concern in Delhi. 'How could Indira and Sanjay sit down and eat with such an uncouth fellow,' wondered one of Mrs Gandhi's pre-election admirers. I think it is at once silly and superficial to attack Sanjay's friendship with Arjun Das on these grounds; indeed, I would commend the association for its egalitarian possibilities. What can and should be attacked is the fact that despite his vastly inferior social status, Arjun Das was typical of the kind of person Sanjay attracted—unscrupulous, venal, vicious, insensitive and slightly stupid. That is the real indictment, not 'rough hands.'

While Sanjay was frolicking around the lawns of Teen Murti in his pedal car, the subject of the 'small car' was, for the first time, raised in India. In Europe and Japan the small car, with its lower petrol consumption and cheaper price, had been a runaway success. Manubhai Shah, a Cabinet Minister in the mid 50s, saw no reason why that success couldn't be repeated in India.

Alas, before the project could be seriously approached it fell into the usual ideological traps. Should it be in the private or public sector? Should it have foreign collaboration or should it be 100 per cent indigenous? So much heat and fervour was exhausted in this academic debate that the original project was left suspended.

The small car came back into national focus quickly, and obliquely. In 1959, the Government set up a Committee, under the Chairmanship of L. K. Jha, to review the state of the automobile industry in the country. Although the small car was not specifically mentioned in its terms of reference, the Committee did state in its report that a 'cheap' car was likely to find widespread acceptance in India. The Jha Committee quantified cheap as Rs. 6,000 and estimated an annual demand of 10,000 vehicles.

Subsequently, the Government invited proposals from potential manufacturers making clear that the recommendations of the Jha Committee would serve as guidelines. Thirteen manufacturers came forward, including the public sector Hindustan Aircraft of Bangalore. Theirs was the most exhaustive project report 'One of the engineer-employees, a young man, successfully produced a prototype made entirely of indigenous material.' At a specially held press conference, this prototype was shown to journalists.

In India committees have a habit of perpetuating more committees. The Government in 1960 appointed yet another committee—this time under the Chairmanship of Mr G. Panday, a retired Chairman of the Railway Board, to study 'the technical feasibility of the idea or the project.' The Panday Committee concluded that the project was indeed feasible, and for execution recommended the French car company, Renault.

Negotiations with Renault began in earnest. However, as the time to sign on the dotted line approached, V. K. Krishnamachari, the then Deputy Chairman of the Planning Commission, burst forth with a string of objections. Krishnamachari was not so much opposed to foreign collaboration as he was to the idea of producing a small car. What India needed, he argued, was not small cars but bicycles, buses, trucks, scooters.

Krishnamachari's opposition was based on priorities. And he seemed to have support in the Cabinet. On August 9, 1962, C. Subramanium, then Minister for Steel and Heavy Industries, stated in the Lok Sabha, '...The small car project cannot be moved up in any list of priorities. The priority in the field of automobiles for some time to come ought to be definitely and overwhelmingly in favour of the manufacturers of commercial vehicles which will provide the base for transport of goods and public transport.'

In the prevailing confusion of private vs public, indigenous vs foreign, low priority vs high priority, Krishna Menon introduced another element. He recommended that the small car be manufactured in defence ordinance factories, and the model he had in mind was the Japanese Toyota.

When Sanjay returned to India with his two-thirds Rolls-Royce apprenticeship, the small car debate was at its zenith. By July 1968, however, one decision had been reached—the car was to be placed in the private sector.

Concurrently, the grapevine in Delhi was thick with rumours about the brave attempts of the Prime Minister's son to put together, in some broken down shed, a prototype of a small car. It was also rumoured that the Planning Commission now favoured the private sector for the small car. This, of course, was a complete reversal of its earlier stand, and critics did not fail to note that the Planning Commission seemed to have changed its mind around the time Sanjay Gandhi entered the small car fray. A coincidence? Mrs Gandhi: 'Some have asked why this car project could not have been taken in the public sector. Firstly, it is not a priority item. Secondly, would the opposition, or those who wish to embarrass me, have been less relentless in their attacks if the public sector had helped Sanjay?'

Sanjay's entry was officially announced on 13 November 1968. The Minister of State for Industrial Development, Raghunath Reddi, announced in the Lok Sabha that among the proposals received for the small car was one by Mr Sanjay Gandhi. The Sanjay proposal, according to the Minister, envisaged the cost to be Rs. 6000, a maximum speed of 53 miles per hour with a consumption of 56 miles to the gallon. Mr Reddi revealed that a total of 14 proposals had been received, including such names as Renault, Citroen, Morris, Mazda, Toyoto, Volkswagen. Renault had quoted Rs. 11,190 while the Japanese had quoted Rs. 6,700 as the price of their models.

'Members of the House,' said a P.T.I. report next morning, 'stirred in their seats' and were 'incensed' as they heard news of Sanjay and the small car.

There was more stirring and more indignation in the coming months. George Fernandes, in his General Secretary of the S.S.P. avatar, summoned the press and accused the Prime Minister of 'practising nepotism of the worst type.'

George noted sardonically that the first act of Mrs Gandhi after assuming the Chairmanship of the Industrial Licensing Committee was to grant a boon to her son for a project which was irrelevant to the needs of the nation. Raj Narain called it 'a disgrace to democracy and socialism'; Jyotirmoy Bosu, 'corruption and nepotism'; Madhu Limaye, 'naked corruption'; Atal Behari Vajpayee, 'corruption unlimited'; S. N. Misra, 'blackmail.'

It was time for Mrs Gandhi to answer back. On 24 September 1970 she declared: 'My son is a delicate young man, and with whatever money and energy he has, he has modelled a car, not a posh one, but one fairly comfortable and suitable to Indian conditions … my son has shown enterprise and I could not say no to him … if he is not encouraged, how can I ask other young men to take risks?'

On 31 November 1970 a Letter of Intent was handed over to Sanjay Gandhi by Mr Dinesh Singh, the Minister of Industries, after a Cabinet discussion on November 9, presided over by the Prime Minister. The Letter of Intent was granted 'on the basis of a paper proposal with no tenders called for and no impartial study' for the mass production of 50,000 'low-priced' cars per year made entirely of indigenous materials. In short, Maruti was licensed to match the total output of the other three domestic car manufacturers.

Besides Sanjay one other applicant, Madan Mohan Rao, was granted a Letter of Intent. 'But Mr Rao got his Letter after his claim had been ignored and after he had approached the Delhi High Court through a writ petition.' Even as the petition was being heard in the court, the Letter of Intent was released and the case withdrawn. Nothing has been heard of Mr Rao since.

Having obtained his Letter of Intent, Sanjay's next objective was land, a plot where he could construct a factory capable of delivering 50,000 vehicles a year.

Bansi Lal had been following the Maruti licence saga with more than neighbourly interest. Beginning as a *'phaticar vakil'* (bankrupt lawyer) he had quickly become Chief Minister of Haryana, thus providing an Indian version of the rags to riches story. One would have thought that he had reached the pinnacle of his ambitions.

This was nowhere near the truth; Bansi Lal had grander visions. Being a wily and scheming politician, he understood that his grand visions would remain illusory unless he was able to ingratiate himself with someone at 1, Safdarjung.

The obvious choice was Indira Gandhi. But toadying to the Prime Minister meant facing competition. There were scores of Bansi Lals in India trying to further their political careers by demonstrating 'unstinting loyalty' to the Prime Minister.

To his credit it must be said that Bansi Lal was the first[5] to spot Sanjay Gandhi as a man of the future, as a man to hitch your bandwagon to. As his initial offering, the Chief Minister of Haryana offered Sanjay choice real estate for his factory, and he offered it at a knock down price.

Bansi Lal made sure his offering was not spurned. Since Sanjay would continue to live with his mother, the plot had to be within driving distance from Delhi. And so it was. Gurgaon district is situated 7 kilometres from Delhi, and the site selected was on the Delhi-Gurgaon highway. Bansi Lal offered Sanjay 296.7 acres of land on this highway.

---

5 Before him, of course, the late L.N. Mishra.

If the land had been lying vacant there would have been no problem, no scandal. As it happened the land was among the most fertile in the state and supported a cluster of villages.

The Sanjay apologists insist that a majority of the people dispossessed by Bansi Lal were retired old men living off their pensions. 'Very few,' claim the apologists, 'were traditional farmers.'

The 'very few', as it turned out, managed to irrigate 90 per cent of the total 405.24 acres requisitioned. There was one tube well for every 25 acres, there were tractors in use, the cattle count was 4 per acre—all of which sustained 1,500 farmers. This was the 'residential' area earmarked for Maruti.

Two other hurdles hovered over the vicinity: an airforce ammunition dump and an airfield. On 11 March 1971 the Commanding Officer of the airfield brought to the notice of the Haryana Government the fact that any construction on the proposed land would constitute a security risk as well as contravene a law which prohibited construction within 1000 metres of the ammunition dump. The factory would also be a flight hazard for planes taking off from and landing on the airstrip. The Commanding Officer, therefore, strongly recommended the cancellation of the requisition order.

Vidya Charan Shukla was then Minister of Defence Production. He entered into a long and acrimonious correspondence with the Commanding Officer. As a token gesture, Shukla had part of the ammunition dump moved elsewhere. The other objections were summarily dismissed.

Compensation was another scandal. Bansi Lal, who was virtually the Haryana Government, snatched the land for Rs. 36 lakhs—Rs. 11,776.42 per acre. (Incidentally, this amount was paid by Maruti to the Haryana government only as late as 1975). Adjacent land, meanwhile, had been sold for as much as Rs. 40,000 per acre. The Rs. 36 lakh compensation was inclusive of standing crops, tube wells and houses in the fields. A member of parliament called the transaction 'daylight robbery'.

The concluding instalment of this unedifying land-grab could easily have been lifted from the traditional feudal-landlord-crushing-helpless-peasant Hindi film.

The farmers of Gurgaon formed a cooperative and went to court in a writ petition contesting the land requisition order. 'The Advocate General of Haryana withdrew the case regarding the acquisition order. The writ became infructuous. The withdrawal was published in the *Gazette* on March 23.' First round then to the farmers of Gurgaon.

The second round, alas, was a knockout, and it went to Bansi Lal. The day after the withdrawal was published, a special acquisition order was issued whose publication was deliberately suppressed for three months. Simultaneously, the villagers were called to court to voice their objections with one proviso: all objections had to be heard in one day and within eight hours.

Suspecting nothing sinister, the villagers went in large numbers. How could they know that the real motive of the objection call was to ensure that 'all the menfolk were away from the villages, so that the police could occupy the land without meeting any physical resistance'? Even as a huge police force was capturing their land, the farmers were being told by the land acquisition officer that they should accept whatever compensation the government pleased to give them, since the land was being acquired in the national interest for 'defence purposes'.

Critics of Maruti received unexpected ammunition when Mr Y. B. Chavan, under fire from the opposition, revealed in the Rajya Sabha that Mr Sanjay Gandhi's income for the year '70-'71, as shown in his income tax returns, was Rs. 722. How, they asked; could an entrepreneur with such ridiculous resources embark on a project of such magnitude? The critics failed to note one vital, hidden Sanjay asset: he was the Prime Minister's son.

A public limited company, Maruti Limited, was floated in the middle of 1971 with Sanjay Gandhi as Managing Director (salary Rs. 4,000 per month plus prerequisites) and three other directors: Mr Raunaq Singh, Mr V. R. Mohan and Mr Vidya Bhushan. M. A. Chidambaram, of Automobile Products of India, was the Chairman.

Whereas Singh, Mohan, Bhushan and Chidambaram had substantial investments in the Company, the Managing Director bought ten shares of Rs. 10 each. To circumvent a stipulation of the Registrar of Companies that a Board Member must own a minimum of 25 shares, the Maruti Board passed a special resolution stating that the minimum share binding was inoperative as far as their company was concerned.

If one examines the private investment of companies and other major shareholders in Maruti, one could almost compile a who's who list of the most disreputable elements in Indian business life. The Minister of State for Home Affairs, R. N. Mirdha, acknowledged as much when, using a typical parliamentary euphemism, he conceded that some of those who had invested in Maruti were 'under pending investigation for economic offences.'

The companies and individual shareholders[6] jostling to put money into Sanjay's small car hoped for two quick gains. Most of them had income tax cases pending against them which they wanted squashed or 'settled', and most of them were in the market for new licences.

A few money details: Maruti Limited began with an authorised capital of Rs. 2.5 crores (by June 1972 it was 10 crores.) In the first year after its inception, shares worth Rs. 25 lakhs were sold, the next year Rs. 68 lakhs and the next Rs. 85 lakhs. The total paid up capital by September 1974 was Rs. 1.8 crores. The value of the net assets of the company as on 31 March 1974 were Rs. 4.5 crores. 52 shareholders had invested a lakh and above.

Besides the big boys, there were numerous small and medium shareholders. Curiously the surnames of these people were either Mishra or Jha. '...the various Mishras are all relatives of the late L. N. Mishra while the Jhas are all relatives of L. N. Mishra's widow. Eight of Mishra's first cousins, nephews and grand-nephews are shareholders. Each of them has 50 to 80 shares of Rs. 1000 each listed against their names. The shareholders also include Mrs Mishra's mother, eight brothers, an aunt, five cousins and two nephews'.

An additional source of income was 'dealership deposits'. In the middle of 1972 Sanjay appointed nearly 75 dealers with the promise that the small car would be delivered within 'six months'. Amounts varying from one to three lakhs were

---

6 Sanjay denies having major shareholders: 'I don't know how you would define a major shareholder. I'd say a major shareholder should have much more than 2 or 3 per cent of the total capital, and we don't have any such people.'

collected from each dealer as deposits. In case of delay, interest commensurate with the bank rate was to be paid. Thus in one year alone ('73-'74), Maruti collected 2.18 crores from its dealers.

Sanjay instructed his dealers to build showrooms suitable for displaying the small cars. Many dealers borrowed the money from banks and pledged their property. Not only did they never see the small car, they received no interest either. A couple of dealers reckless enough to ask for a refund of their deposits during the Emergency were promptly jailed under M.I.S.A. (In May '75 Maruti had the temerity to ask its dealers to collect Rs. 2,000, half of which was to be released to the company, as 'counter security' from potential customers).

For the next four years, while Sanjay was busy in his factory, Mrs Gandhi and the Congress Party were busy facing a spate of criticism both in parliament and in the press over Maruti tangles.

Sanjay did get a breather. A few months after he received his Letter of Intent he went on an European tour as a 'consultant' in a team sponsored by the Chairman of Maruti. He visited car manufacturing units in West Germany, Italy, Britain, Czechoslovakia, without being overly impressed either by their technology or their plants. There was nothing, he said on his return, that Maruti could learn from foreigners.

In November '72, Sanjay unveiled the small car prototype with the news that Maruti would be on the road by April '73. There would be no change in design or performance, only a minor hike in price (actually 90 per cent). Due to an increase in raw material costs, the peoples' car would now be priced at Rs. 11,300.

The increase, it is partially true, was caused by a jump in raw material costs. However, the main reason was inefficient utilization of machinery and resources. What Sanjay was attempting to do was operate a manufacturing unit on a capital of Rs. 6 crores when what was actually required was something like Rs. 60 crores.

He knew this. But where was the additional money to be raised? No more investors seemed to be in sight and his dealers had already forked out exorbitant sums.

He turned to his last source: banks and financial institutions. But here too he was at a disadvantage. Before considering applications for loans, banks demand a project report in which a detailed production plan has been worked out. Sanjay had no project report; nevertheless he did manage to extricate finance.

Word naturally spread. As early as 1972, Congress and Opposition clashed in the Rajya Sabha over Maruti loans. Mr N. K. Shejwalkar of the Jana Sangh, 'stirred up a wave of protest from the ruling party benches by contending that the Industrial Finance Corporation (I.F.C.), a public institution, had loaned a large sum of money to the company' not for sound fiscal reasons but for reasons of political clout. Another Jana Sangh member demanded to know the truth behind the rumour that the I.F.C. had sanctioned to Sanjay 'the biggest loan of the year in a record period of one week.' With masterly evasion Mr Reddi, the Minister under fire, replied: 'I cannot say anything about any loans that a financial institution may have advanced to Maruti. My department is waiting for the first balance sheet of the company.'

Cushioned by official protection, Sanjay began drawing frequently from banks and public institutions by a combination of bluff and blackmail. Two banks, Central and Punjab National, for example, forwarded large chunks of money at reduced interest rates and without the necessary collateral. 'Soon a point was reached when the banking system, including the Reserve Bank of India, could not go on coughing out money to a non-existent project.' The Deputy Director of the Reserve Bank, Dr R. K. Hazari, informed the nationalized banks 'not to advance further money to Maruti'. Hazari also informed the Finance Minister, Subramaniam, of the decision he had taken.

The Chairman of the Central Bank, Taneja, was under particular pressure. Mindful of Hazari's instructions, he kept prevaricating with Sanjay's persistent loan requests. Finally, he had to say 'no'.

Come the Emergency, Taneja was unceremoniously removed, despite protests from bank employees and directors. Hazari also had to go. Meanwhile, the Governor of the Reserve Bank of India, S. Jaganathan was hurriedly retired and in his place K. R. Puri was appointed—solely because he promised to be 'more receptive to loan demands from Maruti'. (At the height of the Emergency, when Sanjay was holding court at 1, Safdarjung, Puri was a frequent visitor. Once when he had been waiting over an hour for an audience, he asked Dhawan to see if 'Mr Gandhi is free now.' Dhawan replied: 'Wait a little longer Mr Puri, after all you have nothing much to do in the office.') Another casualty was R. K. Talwar, a distinguished banker of proven excellence and Chairman of the State Bank of India, who was also resisting demands for overdrafts and loans. Removing him was not as easy as Taneja. A law had to be enacted which empowered the Government to dismiss any Chairman of a nationalized undertaking with three month's notice.

What manner of factory did Sanjay possess? Graham Sargeant (motoring correspondent) and Anthony Mascarenhas of the *Sunday Times*, London visited Maruti in April '77. They discovered: 'The body shop where workers apparently hand-stitched the little Maruti bodies is a joke. So also is the engine shop, the pattern shop and the foundry, and the whole place with three ground level fireplaces looks like a dirty indoor barbecue. It was explained to us by my escort, the works supervisor who formerly supervised a scooter assembly plant elsewhere, that these furnaces were used to melt ingots which were then hand-poured into a single set of engine moulds. Apparently this process caused one of the defects of the Sanjay-designed engine which had a tendency to leak oil after 4,000 kilometres. It also explained why we later found almost the entire Maruti car production—20 finished models and 20 car bodies—abandoned like toys in the centre of the indoor stadium that is the car assembly.'

A car which emerged from such a primitive plant was, to put it mildly, going to have problems on the road. To make ready the first prototype, Sanjay requisitioned a motorcycle engine and tried to adapt it for Maruti. It didn't adapt. The second prototype, on a trial run, turned turtle, the third got overheated too quickly... The car leaked, it made excessive noise, the suspension was faulty, the doors wouldn't close properly, the steering was too light, and it consumed not less but more petrol. Maruti, in early '74, was not a vehicle for a middle-class Indian family but for Buster Keaton and the Keystone Cops.

The façade of normalcy was kept up. In the 1972 World Fair at Delhi a Maruti model was prominently displayed in the Haryana Pavilion as an instance of Indian technology and ingenuity. The car was placed on an elevated, revolving pedestal, its features accentuated by spotlights.

If Sanjay gained good publicity from the World Fair, he gained adverse publicity from the D.M.K. Tamil Nadu Industries Minister, S. Mahadevan. Mahadevan on a visit to Delhi had seen a Maruti—and he was petrified. To him the car looked as if 'it was made of tin'. He sat in the car but insisted it stay stationary: 'I was so scared I did not have the guts to ride in it.' The *Indian Express* headlined Mr Mahadevan's observations under 'TIN (Y) CAR'.

The one man who had accurately evaluated the disaster-potential of Sanjay's Maruti for the Prime Minister was P. N. Haksar. Actually his misgivings went back to 1971 when Sanjay was awarded the Letter of Intent. He couldn't, of course, ask Mrs Gandhi to order her son to abandon a project on which he had been working for seven years. What he did was to recommend to Mrs Gandhi that, in view of the mounting criticism, it might be useful to get a feasibility test done on Maruti. The Vehicles Research and Development Establishment (VRDE) at Ahmednagar was suggested, where Haksar was certain Maruti would fail the test, thus letting Mrs Gandhi off the hook.

Haksar's feasibility suggestion didn't please Sanjay too much. Nevertheless, he agreed and set to work on preparing a test car for Ahmednagar.

The engine had been the principal problem. Sanjay had designed many variations but they never seemed to work. No great admirer of foreigners or their cars, he turned as a last resort to a foreigner, a German engineer called Muller. Muller surreptitiously imported into the country two four-stroke German engines. Madhu Limaye, an old foe of Sanjay and Maruti, somehow got wind of this and dropped a 'bombshell in the House'. He charged that Maruti had not only illegally imported engines but was also planning to alter the 100 per cent indigenous stipulation laid down in the Letter of Intent.

How Maruti passed the feasibility test is a mystery. A car did go to Ahmednagar—some say on top of a truck—and did undergo tests for six weeks. On 30 March 1974 VRDE Ahmednagar issued Maruti a clearance certificate and T.A. Pai announced in Parliament that Maruti had passed the most 'rigorous tests'.

To counter the plethora of hostile publicity dropping all around him, Sanjay launched a brave but unsuccessful public relations campaign to dupe the nation into believing that his small car was making steady and sure progress. Each annual report of the company would exude great confidence, promising that the cars would be in the showrooms 'very soon'.

In 1972 the car was to have been 'presented for sale in the market in the first half of 1973'. In 1973, when Maruti was not presented for sale, the delay was attributed to engine problems. In 1974 Maruti was 'at the threshold of production. The factory building is complete and machinery has started arriving.' In 1975 'steady progress' was being made 'toward the achievement of planned targets' and it was possible to 'start manufacture of Maruti cars on a moderate basis'. In 1976 'the car manufacturing activity was started' but 'taking into consideration a country-wide recession in the automobile industry, your directors have decided to watch the situation before launching mass production of cars'.

A few days after the elections had been announced, Sanjay gave a press conference to the Foreign Press Journalists Association in Delhi, where this interesting exchange transpired.

Q. How is Maruti doing?

A. Okay, we are making progress slowly on the tooling.

Sanjay Gandhi in 1977 was still slowly making progress on tooling for a car which should have been in the market in 1973!

David Selbourne in 'An Eye to India' writes: 'Purchase price, design, specification, engine capacity and licensing period; the dates for the rolling out of the preproduction prototype for road trials, for volume production and the volume itself; number of employees, cost of production, company assets and amount of investment; from 1970 to 1975 were announced, raised, lowered, varied, withdrawn or forgotten.' By the time the Emergency had been announced, Mr Gandhi had asked for the fourth extension on his Letter of Intent and the price of his people's car has escalated from Rs. 6,000 to Rs. 25,000.

Sanjay would probably be loath to admit this, but by the end of '74 he had virtually written off his cherished car project—for financial reasons. The money had run out and there was no prospect of more coming in. Banks, dealers, investors, public institutions had been squeezed to the hilt.

The seriousness of the company's situation was further emphasized when it started selling Maruti alloted cement and steel— two scarce and rationed items—in the open market. Sanjay explains that he was only selling 'scrap', but whoever heard of cement as scrap!

Significantly, no new machinery was installed in the factory after '74; instead, a diversification programme was chalked out— more evidence that the original project had been postponed if not abandoned. In early '74 there was a small notice in the press announcing that Maruti had gone into the business of producing road-rollers; the state of the people's car was not mentioned at all.

As usual, questions were asked in the House by the Opposition, and as usual the ruling party was embarrassed.

During the Emergency, and even before, vague rumours had been heard about allied companies Sanjay had launched. Their workings, however, were shrouded in mystery, not for want of information but because Maruti itself was hogging all the spotlight and attention.

Therefore, the news that seven months prior to floating Maruti Sanjay had registered a private limited company called Maruti Technical Services (MTS) came as something of a surprise. Sanjay's partners in this venture were his sister-in-law (Sonia), his two nephews (Rahul and Priyanka) and one other person named Shroff. Together the Gandhi family owned 99 per cent of the shares of MTS with Sanjay's personal investment of Rs. 1.25 lakhs in a paid-up capital of Rs. 2.15 lakhs.

For someone who could spare only Rs. 100 for the parent company launched seven months later, Sanjay was extraordinarily generous with MTS, as was his brother's family.

Did Sanjay win a sweepstake? Did he come into a secret inheritance from his father or grandfather? Did he touch his mother for a loan? After all, Indira Gandhi was at pains to point out 'that she and her family had made great sacrifices in the interests of the country and did not have any property or assets of their own'. Sanjay's willingness and ability then to invest so much money in MTS might appear baffling on cursory examination.

Not so baffling if you consider why the company was conceived and how it was run.

Consider, first of all, the Managing Director. Sonia Gandhi had no known managerial skills or technical expertise; yet she received a salary of Rs. 2,500 plus one per cent commission on net profit, plus bonus, gratuity, provident fund, medical aid, free travel, house allowance, telephone, car (with driver and petrol).

To provide Sonia Gandhi with a monthly income was not the *raison d'etre* of MTS; it was quite simply to 'milk' the much larger and financially stronger Maruti. A 20 year 'tie-up' between Maruti Technical Services and Maruti Limited was organized, by which the latter agreed to pay the former a yearly minimum of 2 per cent of the value of net sales in return for consultancy services: 'supply of expertise for design, manufacture, and assembly of cars'. To bless the tie-up Maruti initially paid Rs. 5 lakhs to MTS.

In this manner the shareholders of Sanjay's first company were able to recover nearly their entire investment in three months, and within two and a half years they were able to build up reserves of Rs. 3.06 lakhs, 'which makes for a 150 per cent appreciation on the original investment of Rs. 2.15 lakhs.'

Consultancy arrangements are not uncommon; if the quality of the service rendered is high, payments of large sums is also not uncommon. But as far as MTS was concerned there was hardly any consultancy rendered because there was hardly any company to render it. The *modus operandi* in fact was worthy of Graham Greene's *Our Man in Havana*. It was 'to list fictitious names. For if Mohan Talwalkar (fictitious) was employed by Maruti Limited as a technical manager he was also given an identical letter of appointment to Maruti's subsidiary, Maruti Technical Services. When Talwalkar was in doubt concerning a technical point, he would write an official letter to his counterpart in MTS requesting advice. The reply would be signed by T. K. Mohan (Talwalkar, Mohan) and addressed to his alias Mohan Talwalkar giving the required advice and enclosing a bill for services rendered.'

In June '75, by which time MTS had milked over Rs. 10 lakhs from Maruti, yet another company was launched. Maruti Heavy Vehicles (P) Limited, was a subsidiary of the family owned Maruti Technical Services which held 59 per cent of its paid-up capital of Rs. 15 lakhs. Other major shareholders were Om Prakash Modi, K. L. Jalan (Managing Directors) and Sanjay Gandhi.

The new company was registered as a small-scale enterprise and it set to work on manufacturing road rollers. Again a tie-up (this time for 10 years) clause was inserted by which MHV paid a commission of 2 per cent of its net sales to MTS for technical assistance. Like its mentor, MHV was a phantom. It had, according to its own books, machinery worth Rs. 12,231 on which, miraculously, it was able to produce goods worth Rs. 16 lakhs.

The machinery was, nevertheless, adequate for assembly. MHV purchased Perkins and Ford engines from companies which had the import licence, fitted them into old, scrap rollers, applied a coat of paint—and sold them as brand new road rollers. Inspection or quality control checks were never undertaken since all of Sanjay's eager clients were either state governments or corporations, who even managed to ignore the fact that MHV road rollers were 40 per cent more expensive than the ones made by a central government undertaking, 'Jessop'.

By the end of '76 a whole maze of ancillary Maruti activity had proliferated. Sanjay was involved in building bus bodies, he was involved in the selling of chemicals (Quick Flow Polymix), he was involved in steel, he became an agent for foreign multinationals (the two big ones being International Harvesters and Piper Aircraft), he was in the market for the sale of trucks. In the words of a Delhi magazine, he had 'his fingers in many pies'.

It was fantastically easy, if you were Sanjay, to get your fingers in many pies. As the *Washington Post* observed: 'The bureaucrats say they can do nothing. Sanjay calls up Secretaries and says "give the contract to so and so"'. A western diplomat posted in Delhi recalls: 'If you wanted to sell something you had to get in touch with Maruti ... Sanjay took no pains to deny his ability to influence Government decisions." After meeting one foreign manufacturer, Sanjay is reported to have said: 'Yes, yes, I can influence things in your direction because I have a line to the Cabinet Secretariat.' Unfortunately, the election verdict put an end to all of Sanjay's expansion plans. State governments, corporations, municipalities, sycophants cancelled orders through Maruti with the same alacrity with which they had placed them.

It is true that the eve of the Emergency saw the affairs of Maruti in a state of Byzantine complexity; a public scandal whose hydra-headed ramifications subverted banking, civil, criminal and company law, import licensing, marketing, state politics...

Blitz is part of a respectable body of opinion which maintains that it was not the Allahabad High Court judgment but Maruti which forced Mrs Gandhi's hand. '...the Sanjay-Bansi Lal caucus began seriously thinking of another project to save Maruti and its political repercussions, which had begun to threaten the Prime Minister's own career, from the mounting public scandal, and at the same time to draw the enormous funds imperative to the automobile plant. There were secret confabulations which ultimately led to the Emergency as the most effective device to silence parliamentary as well as public criticism.'

One of Mrs Gandhi's advisers told Ian Jack of the London *Sunday Times*: 'Maruti is where the rot started because it raised so many questions that have never before been properly answered.'

My own view is that while Sanjay might have greatly favoured a national situation in which he was overlord, and while Mrs Gandhi was undoubtedly keen in protecting her son from public and parliamentary wrath, it is political nonsense to place the blame for 25 June 1975 on the door of Maruti. What Mrs Gandhi was doing on that day was not protecting her son but herself. Would there have been an Emergency without Jagmohan Sinha and vacation judge Iyer?

You don't have to be a legal or civil or mathematical wizard to detect a distinct pattern in three Maruti companies—Maruti, Maruti Technical Services, Maruti Heavy Vehicles—and their relationship with each other. In this triumvirate the pivot, of course, was Maruti Technical Services. This family-owned company was the money receptacle into which Maruti and to a lesser extent MHV paid in. The labyrinthian capital structures, the façade of legality cannot obscure this single fact. For most of its existence Maruti, a public limited company relying on public funds, did little else but serve as a conduit to enrich MTS. In 1975 when the consultancy arrangement between Maruti and MTS was altered, MHV started drawing funds from Maruti which in turn was passed on to MTS.

The other fact which emerges is that Rajiv Gandhi and his family are contaminated. Possibly, there were occasional fights between the brothers; possibly, Rajiv was not happy with some of the goings -on; possibly, as Rajiv claims, Sanjay got the papers signed from Sonia while he was away from Delhi. All this does not alter the record: till almost the very end Rajiv, Sonia and the kids were involved either as directors or shareholders in MTS and later in MHV.

There are two options open to directors of sinking concerns. They can either sell out or go into liquidation. Both these options were open to Sanjay, and they were rejected for a very private reason.

Selling out, naturally, is only possible if you have buyers— a contingency remote for a company like Maruti making nothing but losses (by December '76, Rs. 2.3 crores). Liquidation, meanwhile, entails a return of moneys collected from various capital constituents—a remote contingency for a company with no real assets to sell.

Nevertheless, both selling and liquidation were within the realm of possibility. Both, however, were acknowledgements of corporate defeat, implicit in which was admission of personal defeat. Sanjay's numerous adversaries would gleefully point out that he had failed despite being heir to a host of privileges: his access to ministers and civil servants, his ability to release scarce raw materials, his capacity to tap money... the final insult his critics would hurl was one they had been hurling since '71— 'Sanjay knows nothing about cars; he is just a spoilt brat who used his mother's name to squander public funds.' As further evidence, the critics would quote the German engineer Muller, whom Sanjay hired in his factory. Muller had said: 'I realized the car couldn't work when Sanjay started to design the engine. He did not know the first thing about designing engines. He had more enthusiasm than ability. He had too much self-confidence, the feeling of being infallible.' Rather than countenance such ego-hurting slights, Sanjay persisted with the myth that one day he would produce the 'people's car.'

David Travinnion, an English apprentice with Sanjay at Crewe, says: 'I read that he had set up a car factory in India. I've studied engineering for seven years and even I wouldn't say I was qualified to design a car. And as for running a factory, I wouldn't have thought he was the sort of person to inspire enthusiasm for working in anyone. He was far too autocratic and I suppose he got worse with the passing of years.'

In the post-election overkill it is being suggested that leave alone a car, Sanjay couldn't put a horse and cart together. My researches suggest otherwise.

Sanjay's car knowledge, by all accounts, is formidable. Someone in the automobile business who knows Sanjay but has no reason to be beholden to him told me: 'He knows a great deal about cars. Whether it is design or fuel or spare parts or new developments in the industry, he is remarkably well informed. He really does love cars. Of course I am not saying that his knowledge was sufficient to run a manufacturing unit.'

For Sanjay, Maruti was a labour of love, an affliction which, paradoxically, proved disastrous, since Sanjay insisted on being involved with even the minutest of details. 'He was running a one-man car factory,' recalls one of Maruti's dealers.

Thus the engine had to be designed by Sanjay, the choice of raw materials, suspension, cooling system, body construction, weight had to be decided by Sanjay. What kind of machinery to install, what personnel to hire were Sanjay's responsibilities. Even the colour schemes had to be Sanjay selected. This kind of personal control and supervision might have been useful if you were making a prototype in a shed, but in an assembly plant officially geared to produce 50,000 vehicles it could only lead to chaos.

What Maruti needed was a team of engineers and designers and technicians with clearly demarcated functions. Sanjay didn't want any of that. He was especially sceptical of people with foreign qualifications or 'too many degrees', people who according to him were 'set in their ideas'. He placed more faith in raw recruits, those who had no ideas at all. With such an insular and parochial attitude, Sanjay proceeded to work on what is universally acknowledged as a highly advanced and technically intricate industry.

Today Maruti mirrors poignantly the fortunes of the Gandhi family. A forlorn and desolate Sanjay has resigned as Managing Director, the bailiffs have come and gone, the workers are on strike, the dealers are demanding their deposits back, the courts have frozen bank accounts (total amount Rs. 25,000), some sensitive records have been burnt, a file is 'missing'; and the Janata Government has appointed an Enquiry Commission. Whatever else might be uncertain in the coming months, one thing is certain: Maruti, the son of the wind god, has been consigned to the back pages of history. A carping historian might, with some justification, contend that 20 finished models—the total output of Maruti in five years—do not deserve even the back pages. The seasoned historian, while sympathetic to the point, will reply that Maruti was not just a story of a car project that failed...

'Future Light of India'

IT IS MOST UNLIKELY that in a pluralistic society you will find a broad-based political party without a youth wing. For two main reasons.

By harbouring a youth wing the party keeps its doors open to those who, having been franchised, are looking for a secure base to rest their political shoulders. A youth wing, additionally, bridges the notorious generation gap, gives the party a cosmopolitan character and refutes charges of antediluvianism. Even though usually no more than ten per cent of the paid-up membership of a party is made up of those under 30, there are sympathizers, part-time workers, drifters—non card-carrying members who deliver the goods when goods require to be delivered.

Secondly, youth wings tend to become the only source of uncontaminated idealism for the party. Certainly, this idealism is sometimes unworldly, naïve, inflexible, but it serves as a useful corrective to the cynicism, power lust and incessant flexibility of the 'veterans'. Mr Peter Hain, a young Liberal of the British Liberal Party, echoed the sentiments of a whole range of young activists when he declared: 'We represent the conscience of the Liberal Party—a conscience that needs to be constantly supervised and goaded.' It is for this reason perhaps that youth wings tend to be ideologically to the Left of the parent body, a situation which can lead to bloody infighting when the parent body itself is avowedly socialist or social democratic.

With a fine disdain for international practice, the pre-Emergeny youth wing[1] of the Congress Party in India had no serious rationale for existence. It had no ideology, very few members, no voice in the higher echelons of power. Consequently, as a pressure group it had virtually no impact. Both the Congress and the Youth Congress were something of a mutual admiration society.

Office bearers did—as office bearers in this country tend to do—proliferate. There was a president, secretary, general secretary, five joint secretaries, treasurers, executive council members, state executive members. The headquarters of the Youth Congress was at No. 10, Janpath in Delhi (the Maruti Commission sits there today) with branches in all state capitals. Once a year, at the annual Congress session, there would be a familial reunion. Youth Congress members would raise their hands to support the majority view, they would lift their pens to sign the majority resolution. In the evening they would

---

1 In May '47 the Indian National Congress started a students' section; but it was only in 1952 that a body called Youth Congress was formed.

entertain the oldies around a campfire with folk dances and 'rural culture'.

With one notable exception: West Bengal[2]. Here under the leadership of Priyaranjan Das Munshi there existed a genuine cadre-based youth organization—'Chhatra Parishad', an instrument nurtured and carved by Munshi himself. Understandably, the allegience of its members was to him as an individual rather than to some distant body in Delhi.

Munshi is typical of Bengali radicalism. A revolutionary who in his spare time writes poetry and has a weakness for the love songs of Tagore, he can also burn and disrupt. 'All Calcutta trembles when Munshi walks' may not be applicable today but in the late 60s and early 70s only a foolish man would dispute that claim. Nevertheless, Munshi's strength is localized, he is the youth leader of West Bengal and certainly politicians there try to keep him in good humour. In the era of Jyoti Basu and the United Front, Mr Munshi and his boys are credited with everything from breaking up meetings to murder. Mr Basu holds the 'Chhatra Parishad' responsible for all the terror in and around Calcutta during the tenure of his first chief ministership; the 'Chhatra Parishad' claims it alone kept the streets of Calcutta safe for women and children to walk. That Mr Munshi was (is) a force to reckon with in West Bengal is incontrovertible, and since the national youth scene was minus any potential leaders, Das Munshi almost automatically found himself the President of the Indian Youth Congress.

The General Secretary of the parent body was Chandrajit Yadav, a card-carrying member of the Communist Party who

---

2 In Kerala, also, the Youth wing of the Congress was fairly active.

had graduated to becoming one of the leading lights of the so-called Left wing of the Congress. Young Ambika Soni was Yadav's protégée, and it was he who asked Munshi if some suitable occupation could be found for this lady of brains and beauty. Before Munshi could answer, Yadav himself suggested: 'Why not make her head of the publications division? She will be good there. She is very intelligent.' So Mrs Soni became head of the publications division of the Youth Congress. A little time elapsed before Yadav ventured: 'Why not give her a title? Why not make her a Joint Secretary?' So Mrs Soni became one of the five Joint Secretaries of the Youth Congress.

Mr Yadav's interest in Ambika Soni's career may have been ignited quite simply by a desire to promote talent. Or did he fall for 'the willowy figure and eyes that sparkled like clusters of fireflies'? Or both? Ambika's personal loyalty to Yadav is beyond question. 'She would double-cross anyone, even Mrs Gandhi, but not him', says Harcharan Singh Josh, an ex-Joint Secretary of the Youth Congress.

Wise and ambitious as she was, Mrs Soni shrewdly grasped the limited capacities of her mentor. He could only push people like Munshi around. Ambika, therefore, opened up a second front and began assiduously to woo Mrs Gandhi, whom she had earlier met in Mexico, where Mr Soni, a foreign service officer, was posted.

Mrs Gandhi, aided no doubt by her famous instincts, took to Ambika immediately, and when the latter returned to India it was only a question of time before she gravitated to the irresistable portals of 1, Safdarjang. Had Mrs Soni relied exclusively on her first mentor it is doubtful if she would have got very far in public life. Thus when critics say Ambika is 'a creation of Mrs Gandhi' they are not wide off the mark.

13 June 1975 was probably Mrs Soni's finest hour. Among the hundreds of rented Indira supporters were a group of young socialists demanding the resignation of the Prime Minister. Ambika thought such a demand patently undemocratic. She went outside the P.M.'s residence in the company of Youth Congress stalwarts and got involved in a squabble. Mrs Soni strongly repudiates slapping or woman-handling or pushing any of the demonstrators. However, a picture appeared in one of the Delhi papers the next day showing her involved in some kind of physical action. It must have warmed the cockles of Mrs Gandhi's heart to see such a young and fiery defender of her interests.

Mid-day June 12 saw Sanjay in the driver's seat. When, just after ten, Mrs Gandhi's private secretary (Seshan) hurried in with the 'unseated' message, Sanjay was in his factory at Gurgaon. He returned before lunch (his usual time), and from then on it would be reasonably accurate to say that he took over the show.

A crisis of this kind brought out the best in Sanjay. Demonstrations, not only outside 1, Safdarjung, but all over Delhi had to be organized quickly; Chief Ministers had to be geared up for action in the states; Press, A.I.R., Doordarshan had to be slanted, resolutions of support had to be circulated and signed. The whole country had to be galvanized into synthetic activity to demonstrate that Jagmohan Lal Sinha's judgement was part of a national 'conspiracy' to unseat his mother.

Events, however, were catching up with him. The election results from Gujarat suggested a halt in the 'Indira wave' while J.P.'s movement, already gaining momentum on a crusade of probity in public life, now received further fillip. How can a government be cleansed if the rot begins at the top? How could a person found guilty of corrupt election practices by a High Court and debarred from holding elective office for six years continue to sit in the Prime Minister's chair?

What disturbed Sanjay most was the press—an estate he had over the years come to despise and distrust. He couldn't understand why it was 'giving so much space' to the opposition, why it was being 'very difficult.' 'He didn't realize,' observed a foreign journalist, 'that in a situation like this it is the opposition which is making the running, and therefore making the news—news which the press reports.' This journalistic priority made no sense to Sanjay; he saw darker forces at work.

The composition of the caucus at this juncture was: Bansi Lal, R. K. Dhawan and, of course, Sanjay. All three were convinced that the quickest way to defuse the mounting agitation was by (a) curbing the press and (b) arresting the front line opposition leaders. This then was Sanjay's mini-Emergency to save his mother, and he formulated it around June 15.

The mother, meanwhile, was preoccupied with her legal and moral standing in the country. Arrogant and haughty as she was, she nevertheless courted public opinion, which, as it was reflected then, suggested she step down temporarily, win her appeal in the Supreme Court, and then step back with all the flourish of someone who has been handsomely vindicated. At one stroke she would manifest her innocence and also her respect for the law of the land. To ensure her safe return, she could select a political dummy, someone guaranteed to give way at the right time. Mrs Gandhi discussed her stepping down ideas with a few of her colleagues and they not only concurred but congratulated her for statesmanship.

Sanjay, on the other hand, thought his mother's plan crazy. He argued that if she ever 'stepped down' she would never 'step up' again. He reminded her that an appeal in the Supreme Court could take six months, even a year—and she knew six months was a long time in politics. Could she be absolutely certain that Jagjivan Ram or Chavan or Swaran Singh or Kamlapati Tripathi—the suggested names for the interim prime minister—would welcome her back once her appeal had been heard? And supposing she lost?

Political pundits argue vociferously that Mrs Gandhi's biggest political miscalculation was not resigning on June 12. Had she done so there would have been no Emergency, no Janata Party, no electoral humiliation. It is, no doubt, easy to be wiser by hindsight, but I believe Sanjay's advice to his mother was at once shrewd and sagacious. By voluntarily resigning on June 12 Mrs Gandhi, for all the reasons advanced by Sanjay, would have committed political harakiri.

Resigning, I suspect, was a bit of a charade anyway. Mrs Gandhi never seriously contemplated abdication. Following a well-established Nehru habit, she was 'thinking aloud', enumerating the options open to her. Thus when Sanjay advocated 'fighting it out' she was easily persuaded. 'But what can I do?' she asked.

Now Sanjay unfolded his mini-Emergency plan. All the trouble, he told his mother, was the work of fifty or so opposition leaders and some sections of the press. Curb them and your problems are over.

Being a pragmatist, Mrs Gandhi enquired about feasibility. Bansi Lal was deputed to investigate, and also to sound out cabinet ministers and chief ministers. The Defence Minister took on the assignment eagerly but said he would not talk to 'those communists'—Nandini Satpathy and Siddharth Shankar Ray.

The culmination of support festivities for the Prime Minister was celebrated at the Boat Club in Delhi. Mrs Gandhi addressed a 'mammoth meeting' (estimated audience 10 lakhs) and except for her two grandsons the entire clan sat neatly behind her. Hand raised in the air, voice threatening to break, she made her indictment: 'My opponents are not only after my chair, they want to murder me and my family.' In her nine years in power Mrs Gandhi had never before displayed her sons and their wives on a public platform. On June 20, she did, and in the process gave a lie to her earlier assertion that only she was in politics, not her family. (Borooah watchers might be interested to note that it was at this rally that he produced his first poetic effort: 'Indira tera subah ki jai, tere sham ki jai, tere kaam ki jai, tere naam ki jai.')

The next morning Sanjay discovered that the Boat Club rally bad been indifferently covered—actually it had not—on TV. A really efficient and loyal minister, according to him, would have ensured a live, full-length telecast from the grounds, but Gujral was 'soft'—and he had been a Communist. Sanjay felt, perhaps rightly, that if the press had to be tamed Inder Gujral was entirely the wrong man to do it. He had numerous friends in the journalistic world, some of whom called him by his first name, and he also believed in archaic concepts like free speech. It is significant that when Sanjay was asked why Shukla had been chosen as Gujral's successor he replied: 'He (Shukla) was good at bandobusti.' Inder Gujral obviously was not.

As is his wont, Sanjay denies having a hand in the unceremonious sacking of I. K. Gujral, which followed less than a week after the Boat Club rally. He denies reprimanding the Minister for 'not doing enough', and he also denies having telephoned Gujral to find out why there was no live coverage of the rally. Mr Gandhi doth deny too much.

Bansi Lal, busy on his rounds eliciting responses to Sanjay's mini-Emergency, found no dissenters. However, almost everyone wanted to know: 'How are you going to do it?' Bansi Lal had a ready answer. The P.M. was going to take on extra-constitutional powers, if need be with the help of the army, which he boasted was 'under his *joti* (shoe).'

Mrs Gandhi was pleased with the first part of Bansi Lal's report. Her cabinet colleagues and chief ministers were with her if she arrested opposition leaders and suppressed the press. That this would have to be done by assuming extra-constitutional powers did not please her. 'We must try to do it within the constitution,' she insisted. The façade of legality was important to her.

On June 24 Krishna Iyer gave Mrs Gandhi only a 'conditional' stay in the Supreme Court, Siddharth Shankar Ray produced a 'constitutional' internal[3] emergency, and late at night on June 25 police all over the country knocked on various doors.

A euphoric Indira Gandhi woke the next morning to find everything had gone just as Sanjay had predicted. Most of the opposition leaders had been apprehended and gone quietly to jail, the press had stopped its 'character assassinations', there were no morchas outside her house, or anywhere else. All was calm and peaceful. Indira's respect for the political wisdom of her son escalated.

---

3 An 'external' emergency already existed.

SANJAY NEVER LIKED DAS Munshi. He was too independent, too conceited, too powerful. 'Between June 12 and 15, which were the vital days,' says Josh, 'unfortunately Munshi could not be in the capital and by the time he arrived Sanjay had already decided who was going to do what. Sanjay also felt Munshi should have been more forceful in his support for Mrs Gandhi after the Allahabad judgement.'

On July 4, Sanjay and Munshi had an amiable first meeting, with the latter reassuring the former that his support for the Prime Minister had been anything but lukewarm. In the course of their conversation Munshi casually mentioned that he was currently busy appointing new Youth Congress office bearers in certain states. Sanjay said he thought the induction of fresh blood a good idea. 'Before you make any appointments,' Sanjay told Munshi, 'you must consult Sitaram Kesari (Bihar), Raghuramhiah (Andhra) and P. C. Sethi (M.P.).'

Munshi was not a great consulter of human beings at the best of times. Moreover, he had his own power equations to satisfy. Nevertheless, he did consult the people Sanjay had suggested only to find that if, for example, Raghuramhiah approved of a name, Vengal Rao didn't. He was caught in an embarrassing cross-fire. Eventually he fell back on the oldest compromise. In Bihar, for instance, he appointed some of Ghaffoor's men, some of Kesari's and some of his own. An unhappy solution, for Munshi alienated all those he had originally set out to please—especially Sanjay, whose worst fears about the Youth Congress President were now confirmed.

The Janata Party assertion that Sanjay collared the government machinery on 26 June 1975 and released it on 21 March 1977 is a piece of forgiveable exaggeration. Mr Gandhi, in fact, moved stealthily, operating for the first six months of the Emergency more often behind the scenes than in front. He had, one must remember, a troublesome car factory to run, and he was also trying to find his feet on a vastly changed political ground. How should he manipulate his national entry? Should he join the Congress? Could a by-election be organized? Perhaps the Youth Congress would be the best forum? With virtually all options open to him, he was like a child with a hundred rupee note in a sweet shop.

Sanjay's acquaintance with his country was, at best, superficial; he hadn't travelled much, and one of his friends says he 'had never seen a village.' However, he knew Delhi intimately, and what he saw he didn't like. Treeless roads, proliferating slums, illegal tenements, poor sanitation, rude taxi-drivers, inefficient public transport, few playing grounds or parks....in short, all the urban ills.

Six civic bodies claimed responsibility for the social welfare of the Union territory: the Delhi Metropolitan Council, the Delhi Administration, Delhi Municipal Corporation, New Delhi Municipal Committee, the Delhi Development Authority, the Delhi Transport Corporation. Singly and collectively their record was dismal. Recalls one official: 'There was no one to get us moving, no leadership—and too much petty inter-departmental fighting.' With Sanjay moving in, leadership problems were solved, and since he was the Prime Minister's son 'things got done.' 'Before' says the same official, 'even if we had to demolish one house it would take us months, sometimes years to get a legal order.'

Sanjay made sure that the senior officials in these civic bodies were men he 'could get on with'. Some officials just trimmed their sails to suit the new Sanjay wind while others were brought in specifically 'because they were effective' i.e.

loyal to Sanjay. Among those who were effective were Kishen Chand, Navin Chawla, B. R. Tamta, Jagmohan, Sushil Kumar, U. S. Ailwadi, A. Biswas, U. S. Srivastava, Dr O. P. Sharma, Radha Raman. Presently most of these gentlemen have either resigned or they are 'on long leave.'

Sanjay's 'moving in' was greatly facilitated by his mother. Knowing her son's interest in the civic affairs of the capital, she bequeathed him control over the city. Enquiries and requests would be channelled by her with the 'why not see Sanjay' gambit. Soon word got around: the P.M. herself wanted all matters pertaining to Delhi to be handled by her son.

In August '75, Sanjay again hit the headlines, and again embarrassed his mother.

A Delhi journalist, Uma Vasudev, who had earlier written an adulatory biography of Mrs Gandhi, approached Sanjay for an interview. Mrs Vasudev edited an ailing magazine called 'Surge' and she thought an exclusive interview with the Prime Minister's son was just the tonic her paper needed.

Uma had long sessions with Sanjay; she visited the Maruti factory, took photographs, sat in the car, and finally produced a comprehensive question and answer interview titled 'Sanjay Gandhi: Man, Myth and Maruti'. As per arrangements, she forwarded a transcript of the interview which Sanjay cleaned up 'removing some four-letter words'. Uma re-submitted a fresh manuscript, Sanjay approved and himself had it passed by the censor. Mrs Vasudev had a scoop on her hands.

It is customary for newspapers and magazines, if they have a big story, to release pre-publication texts to the wire services. Mrs Vasudev sent copies of the interview to U.N.I., P.T.I, and Reuters. All three picked up the one passage which was 'news.' While passionately advocating free enterprise Sanjay, unprovoked, lashed out on the communists: '... if you take all the people in the Communist Party, the big wigs—even the not so big wigs— I don't think you'd find richer or more corrupt people anywhere.'

The next morning when this blast appeared 'the Communist Party of India was up in arms, ninety papers in the U.S. had published excerpts of the interview, and it was out in British and European papers in the earliest editions ... the political repercussions were immediate,' records Mrs Vasudev in her subsequent book, 'Two Faces of Indira Gandhi.'

While these political repercussions were raging, Mrs Gandhi was out surveying flood-hit areas in Haryana. She returned on the evening of August 28 and immediately passed orders that the interview which condemned her electoral allies should be suppressed; Sanjay next morning issued the usual I-didn't-really-mean-it denial, and Uma Vasudev was told she couldn't carry the prized interview in her magazine. If there is a moral or two in this unhappy tale it is that journalists shouldn't get their copy vetted by prime minister's sons, and if they have a really big story they should print it in their own papers first—and let others pick it up from there.

Even though Sanjay Gandhi was working under the lantern, the enormous power he wielded was apparent to those in the inner circle. They also appreciated that that power would be transferred to whatever group he was identified with.

One group trying desperately to secure Sanjay's patronage was the Youth Congress in Delhi. 'We wanted him because he would be good for us; it's always good to have power on your side,' says Josh. The overtures were reinforced by Ambika Soni directly and through R. K. Dhawan. Mrs Soni coveted the President's post for herself which she knew would only fall vacant if Sanjay joined hands with her. Mr Gandhi needed little encouragement for this battle; he had his own score to settle with Munshi.

In September Sanjay revealed his true strength. He ordered all the state Youth Congress presidents to assemble for a meeting in Delhi. There was no cause for them to accept the invitation— Sanjay was then not even a member of the Youth Congress! On what authority was he inviting them to the capital? Naturally they came, and for good measure the Congress General Secretary, P. V. Narsimha, put in an appearance too. No specific mention was made of personalities or of changing personnel. Instead, Sanjay lectured the state presidents on what he thought should be the goals and aspirations of the Youth Congress. 'He was very clear on what he wanted, and he spoke with tremendous authority,' remembers Ashok Nigam, the then General Secretary of the Delhi Youth Congress.

Sanjay by now had come to the crossroads of his career. He couldn't continue to sit in his mother's house and pull strings. He needed visibility, an official status, something which would be an improvement on 'Prime Minister's son'. R. K. Dhawan urged him to accept the Youth Congress offer. No one would be able to accuse his mother of nepotism since it was entirely natural for a conscientious young man of 28 to work through a youth party.

Munshi, of course, had to be removed first. He would never accept subservience. Sanjay would either have to work under him or with him. Both alternatives were unacceptable.

On 8 November Priyaranjan Das Munshi met Mrs Gandhi briefly. He had been ordered to Delhi by the P.M., and he knew she was going to ask for his head. Eschewing preliminaria, Mrs Gandhi immediately reeled off complaints against the Youth

Congress, the main charge being its poor contribution in helping to implement her wonderful 20-point programme. 'I think you should resign' said Mrs Gandhi. Munshi resigned.

At an extraordinary meeting of the Youth Congress on 9 December 1975, two important portfolios were filled. Ambika Soni took over Munshi's job and Sanjay was appointed to the Executive Council. Both appointments, according to Ashok Nigam, were unconstitutional. 'Only a meeting of national delegates, held once every two years, could take such decisions. Sanjay was not voted into the Executive—he was co-opted.'

Why had Sanjay joined the Youth Congress and not the Congress? 'The Youth Congress was Congress' most disorganized and exploited wing. The youth in India have tremendous energy and enthusiasm. If this energy and enthusiasm can be channelized to do constructive work, it would give the youth a sense of achievement and go a long way in the task of building the nation. The Youth Congress should not confine itself to the politically committed young men and women but should also encourage young professionals, artists, writers and farmers to join in the task.'

Some surprise was expressed when Sanjay did not pitch for the presidency—which was his for the asking. But Sanjay had other, bigger plans. As the *New York Times* speculated: 'The appointment of Mr Gandhi in the Youth Congress is seen as a first step towards a major post in the party or possibly in the Government.' Sanjay had no wish to get bogged down in a job he might have difficulty shedding. Presidents have terms of office and so do Executive Members, but it is easier to resign from the latter. Moreover, with a pliable President like Ambika Soni, executive membership was enough to control the organization. As Ashok Nigam recalls: 'It was not Ambika but

Sanjay who was President ... it became quickly apparent that the only possible relationship was that of employee to boss.'

Ambika had her own ideas. She envisaged that once Sanjay was on the executive wing she would be able to shelve him or at least contain him. He was a young boy who would be happy with a bit of flattery and publicity. Meanwhile, the organization would be securely in her hands—a calculation disproved one day after Ambika assumed office.

Jagdish Luthra, a U.N.I. reporter, was sent to interview Sanjay. After a brief chat, Luthra asked Sanjay who he should contact in future regarding Youth Congress matters. Sanjay pressed his buzzer, whispered something into the ears of a peon, and presently Ambika Soni arrived. 'Her,' said Sanjay, 'contact her.' Luthra remembers the resentment on Mrs Soni's face. 'She was livid at being treated like a clerk. I could see she didn't like it. She left the room immediately.'

Mrs Soni says she consumed the first few months of her tenure as President 'sorting out the mess' left by her predecessor. She claims no records were kept, there were no files, no printed forms, no tabulation of accounts or funds; internal administration was in shambles. Working singly, sometimes '12 hours a day' she got the organization working again.

Sanjay played no part in the cleaning up activity. He was greatly perturbed about numerical strength. The total membership of the Youth Congress, he had discovered, was a miserly seven lakhs. If he was going to use 'the Youth Congress as a national platform from which to bully the senior leadership of the Congress Party itself and thus pave the way for himself as the next national leader', he would need many more heads.

A massive and urgent recruitment campaign was launched. Anyone under 35 and in possession of one rupee was eligible.

Previously, there had been some kind of scrutiny, some kind of screening, but Sanjay was so completely determined to swell membership as fast as possible that all procedural formalities were dropped. Only talk of 'crash membership' was heard.

And, of course, there were hundreds and thousands eager to crash in—now that Sanjay Gandhi was in their midst. Not only were procedural formalities ignored, the age restriction too became flexible. Shopkeepers in Delhi remember greying and balding men flaunting Youth Congress badges and cards. 'Who could question them?' they say.

The over 35s were not the real cause of the evil that later flourished and prospered under the name of Youth Congress. The evil was what the Youth Congress quickly became: 'an umbrella organization which sheltered a variety of goondas, thugs, pick-pockets, criminals'—all the 'bad characters' and 'antisocial' elements police usually keep a record of.

In June the Delhi police arrested a pimp who had become a problem. Many complaints from 'members of the public' about this 'nuisance' had been received. Usually the law turns a blind eye to small-time operators, but this one was becoming too big for his chappals. A couple of days in the cooler would straighten him up. Two constables were sent to pick him up.

'You can't arrest me,' said the man.

'Why not?' asked the constable.

'I am Youth Congress.'

'But till yesterday you were a pimp.'

'That was yesterday. Today I am Youth Congress.'

The police had to let him go.

With such indiscriminate enrolling, membership was bound to perk up. Indeed, by February '77, the figure had jumped from seven to sixty lakhs. Sanjay did not care how or why. He was just delighted to be leading a body with such a large following. Now he spoke for a national youth movement. But at what expense? Even Mrs Soni admitted: 'The Youth Congress had been infiltrated by hoodlums and gangsters... If anybody says no excesses were committed by the so-called Youth Congress members he would be a liar.'

Mr Sanjay Gandhi's gala public appearance was synchronized with the 75th Plenary Session of the All India National Congress held at Komagatu Maru Nagar. This is how he was observed in the papers: 'Neatly dressed in spotless white khaddar and pyjama, he uninhibitedly mixed with the youth and the office bearers of the Youth Congress... He moved briskly, followed by enthusiastic groups of young men and women from the pandal to the smaller shamianas... He was easily accessible to party workers who wanted to see him... In none of his speeches did he refer to any "isms". His accent was on constructive work.' Ashok Nigam, who attended many Youth Congress 'planning' meetings, confirms: 'Any discussion of ideology was made taboo.'

The 'new wave' in Indian politics had made his presence felt (where was the mother?). He spoke at various cell meetings expounding the benefits and opportunities the Emergency presented to the nation. 'Go to the villages and serve rural India,' he advised his followers. They cheered enthusiastically and 'gave him a standing ovation.'

At the conclusion of the session, several thousand Youth Congress members led by Sanjay took an eclectic pledge: 'I shall promote the ideals of democracy, socialism, secularism and nationalism. I shall fight the political evils of modernization (sic), fascism and national chauvinism... the economic evils of property ownership and all means of production, exploitation and inequality ... the social evils of casteism, communalism, male chauvinism and oppression of women, child marriage and the dowry system ... the cultural evils of elitism, imitation of foreign models, illiteracy, religious bigotry, dogmatism and spiritualism.' Having taken on so much, it is not surprising that the Youth Congress achieved so little.

Once the Komagatu Maru session was over Sanjay came out into the open. And an incredible series of journeys began which encompassed the length and breadth of the country. He would be in Bombay on Monday, in Bhopal on Wednesday, in Lucknow on Thursday, in Bangalore on Friday and on Saturday afternoon he would be in Hyderabad.

On a visit to Jaipur, Sanjay was welcomed at the airport by the Chief Minister, the Rajasthan Cabinet, Youth Congress leaders, senior state officials, social workers and 'eminent personalities of the city'. The *Times of India* observed: 'Overnight, the city was transformed. It was swathed in a splash of colour. Decorative gates and welcome arches sprang up as if out of nowhere. There were 501 of them, each of distinctive design. A silvery archway covered a long flyover from end to end.'

It is now known that at least a thousand buses were requisitioned to bring in the 1,00,000 listeners. Mr Gandhi, as usual, softly chided the Chief Minister for arranging the extravagant show (one he secretly enjoyed) which had cost an estimated Rs. 50 lakhs.

The reception Sanjay received in Jaipur was typical of the reception he received at most capitals. In Lucknow, if *Current* is to be believed, 'Mr Gandhi attended no less than eight functions spread over 12 hours and over hundred miles... Before the day could break out, villagers trekked long distances to line both sides of his lengthy route. Women with children in their laps, students armed with conch shells and old men with hope and pride in their eyes turned up by the thousands to meet hamar betua (our son).'

To keep pace with his mother, Sanjay formulated his personal five-point plan (originally four): family planning, tree planting, abolition of caste and dowry systems, eradication of illiteracy and slum clearance. Together, these five points constituted a programme which was immediately hailed as the charter of a 'cultural revolution' in India.

Sanjay's five-point panacea, as Martin Woollacott indicated in the *Guardian*, 'was unexceptionable in itself... The worst aspect was the simple-minded and mechanistic way in which the aims were perceived. Nevertheless, it is also true that the simplicity of the slogans and quick results promised did enlist the energies and idealism of many young, middle-class men and women.'

Not only was the programme unexceptionable, it was cleverly apolitical. None of the points in the programme impinged directly on what we in India understand as 'politics'. Perhaps it was fitting for a man who had once said he 'found politics very boring' to identify himself with a 'revolution' that was social rather than political. (That you couldn't have one without the other was beyond Sanjay's comprehension.)

Equipped with a separate programme, the Youth Congress for once found itself possessed with aims and objectives—plus political clout. Originally the idea had been that the Youth Congress would work in conjunction with the state Congress, and together they would usher in whatever new era mother and son envisaged for the country. In practice it didn't work out that way. The Youth Congress, inebriated on power, soon began functioning as an autonomous unit, frequently riding roughshod over state governments. No Chief Minister—with the exception of Nandini Satpathy and S. S. Ray—had the courage to control or question the young men who claimed to be working for Sanjay and Ambika. The Congress President himself declared: 'The emergence of Sanjay Gandhi as the youth leader has electrified the atmosphere in the country. Our generation is dying out. It is time the youth take over.' In most states of India they did precisely that.

To emphasize the pre-eminence of his organization, Sanjay would declare to his audiences on state visits: 'You must always ask the Youth Congress to redress your grievances.' The unfortunate Chief Minister, invariably next to Sanjay, cheered lustily.

By talking to the protagonists, it is virtually impossible to arrive at any realistic conclusion about the work done by the Youth Congress. Ambika Soni argues that 'the results we have achieved are staggering' while a taxi driver of Delhi told me in September '76: 'Youth Congress? I call it the "Goonda Congress". My own view is that more was achieved on paper than in reality.

These are the gains Sanjay lists under the name of Youth Congress in Delhi: '20,000 residential plots for Janata, low and middle income groups; 21 new resettlement colonies in different parts of Delhi for resettlement of squatters/jhuggi jhopri dwellers; 4,000 houses constructed by the D.D.A.; general living conditions improved in (a) redevelopment of Jama Masjid complex (b) shifting of iron merchants market—Lohar Mandi (c) shifting of old motor part dealers/kabaris—Motia Khan (d) shifting of Lakkar Mandi (e) shifting of cycle market (f) shifting of wholesale fruit and vegetable market—Sabzi Mandi; a model village of Katwarai Sarai has been redeveloped; about 40,000 heads of cattle have been removed from urban areas; firm action to eliminate stray dogs has been taken.'

I met Jagdish Tytler, ex-President of the Delhi Youth Congress, and he inundated me with 'facts and figures' on adult literacy classes, legal aid cells and marriage counselling initiated under the aegis of the Youth Congress. And there is no denying that some of these centres and cells did exist, and they did do the work assigned to them.

However, let's just examine the village, Katwaria Saria, which Sanjay claims was redeveloped by the Youth Congress. A national weekly which investigated this redevelopment reports: 'We met a General Secretary of the Indian Youth Congress who told us about a village they had adopted. When we pressed him for details he directed us to the President of the Delhi unit. We tracked down the President to his office where he was extremely busy dealing with an astonishing variety of cases—from an aggrieved school-teacher, a wronged housewife, to an entrepreneur who was frustrated with the bureacracy. He told us such a village existed, but he couldn't recall its name. He directed us to a lecturer who he said was directly involved with the project. We called this person on the telephone and he admitted that he was heading the committee which directed the project. The name of the village? He would have to find out, he said. Finally it turned out that the village in question *did* exist but the project had nothing to do with the Youth Congress.'

Redeveloping mythical villages is not what the Youth Congress is remembered for in Delhi; a more permanent memory is of Youth Congress workers hounding and subverting almost the entire commercial life in the city.

Armed with Y.C. badges, groups of young and not-so-young people would press shopkeepers for 'donations'. Sometimes the donation would be for an advertisement in a forthcoming souvenir (which was never forthcoming), sometimes for an adult literacy centre, sometimes for a family planning centre, and sometimes a straight donation. 'Whenever I saw these ruffians,' says a sports dealer in Connaught Place, 'I thought my god how much will I have to give out this time. I must be honest. I always gave. My only interest was to get rid of them—for that day at least.'

Such harassment became an almost daily feature. The Youth Congress boys always found some pretext to extort. Perhaps the poor shopkeeper had not properly displayed the mandatory price tags, perhaps he had not put up the mandatory board listing his stocks, perhaps he had not reduced prices by the mandatory ten per cent. 'Donate Rs. 100 or we'll call the police' was the customary threat.

After getting my chappals polished opposite Odeon cinema, I gave the boy his 50 paise. He returned 10 paise back and pointed to a barely readable scrawl on his box: 'Shine reduced by 20-point programme'. All over Delhi, shops, hotels, restaurants were plastered with pictures of Indira Gandhi which bore proud notices: 'In keeping with the 20-point programme we have reduced prices by. . . .' Says Joshi: 'At least half the people going around collecting money on behalf of the Youth Congress were not even remotely connected with the organization,' Little wonder then that on the night of the election results the Delhi Traders Association, which had earlier thrown its weight and money behind the Janata, took out a special victory morcha to celebrate freedom from Youth Congress tyranny.

And then Turkman Gate.

Like all civilized and sensitive human beings, Sanjay abhorred slums. They were ugly, a breeding ground for disease and delinquency, an insult to a sovereign, independent nation. Sanjay's civilized notions went further. He believed people lived in slums not because of economic impoverishment but because they were lazy—perhaps they even enjoyed living there. Left to their own devices they would continue to live in squalor. What these people needed was a bit of government stick.

Coupled with this belief was a middle-class detestion of degradation not for reasons of humanity but because slums were an eyesore and they sullied the landscape of an otherwise neat city. Besides, what would the tourists say?

Sanjay was not concerned with the problems of slums or even with eradicating them. He was concerned with getting them out of sight—some place remote where, hopefully, no one could see them. Then he could say he had 'beautified' Delhi.

Turkman Gate was one big slum. I don't think anybody would deny that. And I am positive the inhabitants would have welcomed the opportunity to live in more congenial surroundings. But Turkman Gate was not a slum which had grown overnight; it had grown over decades. Families had been born there and had died there, and so even in a ghetto there existed a complete fabric of community life. The people who lived in this slum were mainly Muslims and among the most destitute. Labourers, rickshawalas, coolies, they lived literally from day to day. If one offered to 'resettle' the wretched of the earth, would they riot?

It all began on the morning of 13 April 1976. A single bulldozer 'started eating its first morsel'—a transit camp on

Asaf Ali Road. This camp had been in existence since '65 and its destruction was taken by the citizens of Turkman Gate with laudible equanimity, even though there were reports that the people of the camp 'were carted out in trucks and dumped into the wilderness where the only comforts were the bold yellow boards marked "facilities".'

The major mystery then was the next D.D.A. move. Would they be satisfied with the transit camp, or would they come back for more? With the demolition of the transit camp complete on April 14, a sense of relief prevailed. Perhaps it was all over? But that very night Akbar, a Youth Congress worker, and his friend Mehboob Ali discovered two D.D.A. men 'hovering around the Badi Masjid of Turkman Gate. They were talking and arguing. One of them was taking down notes.'

The morning of the 15th saw the reappearance of the dreaded bulldozer—not one, but two. A hostile crowd gathered.

'We only want to break the footpaths', said the D.D.A. official.

'But you don't need bulldozers to break footpaths' shouted the crowd.

'I assure you no houses will be demolished. We will break only the foothpath.'

Such assurances were no longer meaningful. The people of Turkman Gate had guessed the real purpose of the bulldozers. A small committee under the veteran local leader Qyamuddin was quickly formed, and they spent the next three days petitioning and pleading. They met H. K. L. Bhagat, Union Works and Housing Minister, who told them their fears were baseless. They met Rukhsana Sultana who promised to intervene only if a family planning clinic was set up at Turkman

Gate and '300 volunteers supplied within the week.' They met Arjun Das who professed complete surprise: he wasn't aware of any demolition around Turkman Gate. They met V. C. Shukla who telephoned a senior D.D.A. official and extracted a promise that the 'bulldozers would be pulled back'. They met Subhadra Joshi, the local M.P., and she too promised all assistance. They met the Chairman of the D.D.A., Jagmohan, and he for a change warned that the consequences of resisting demolition 'will be serious.' They met Sanjay Gandhi and presented him a memorandum with 1,000 signatures. 'He greeted them coldly...nodded when the meeting was over.' They met Executive Counsellor Radha Raman: 'I am ignorant of any demolition plans', he said.

Of all the people the committee had met, the one person who was not ignorant of demolition plans was the Punjabi Chairman of the Delhi Development Authority (D.D.A.), Jagmohan—an intelligent, shrewd and dangerously ambitious reactionary whose motives for uprooting lakhs of people were as much communal as they were selfish. Jagmohan did seriously consider Turkman Gate a fifth column, a 'second Pakistan', and he was determined to disperse it. During the Emergency Mr Jagmohan became one of the whizkids of Sanjay's court. For services rendered to Mr Gandhi and the nation he was awarded the Padma Bhushan. Endorsing the award, *Blitz* said: 'His greatest single achievement was the shifting of seven lakh jhuggi dwellers to new resettlement colonies in a record time of eight months.' Jagmohan never came forward to collect his honour, the election results saw to that. And if we are to apportion blame for the barbarity, callousness and cruelty of Turkman Gate, the man to nail is Jagmohan.

Adjacent to Turkman Gate is a three-star hotel called Ranjit, where on the evening of April 18, Sanjay, Jagmohan, Ramesh Datta (leader of the 'Nehru Brigade') and two unidentified women were 'conferring' in a room. Word of this conference got around, and Qyamuddin with three others set off again to make a last-ditch plea. 'After an hour the four came back carrying a strange tale. They had managed to push their way past the waiters into the suite... Sanjay Gandhi shrank back as soon as he saw them. He raised a questioning eyebrow at Jagmohan. The latter was furious. "I have already talked to you in the morning. How dare you come and disturb me", he screamed. The four residents tried meekly to ask for an assurance that the bulldozers would not come back tomorrow. But they were interrupted by the Nehru Brigade leader. "I give you exactly five seconds to get out of this room or I will have you thrown out" the Nehru Brigade leader ordered imperiously. Intimidated, the four ran away.'

Sanjay scoffs at the Ranjit hotel story. 'I was not even in Delhi—I was in Simla', he says. It is difficult to believe that this graphically described incident is entirely the work of fertile and motivated imaginations. Sanjay did go to Simla, but he left immediately after, not before, the riot. If one examines the daily press between April 20 and May 1, Sanjay's name is conspicuously absent. Probably he had been advised by his mother to lie low for some time—and this was precisely what he was doing in Simla.

Even if Sanjay was in Simla when the riot broke, does that diminish his responsibility? Are we to understand that Jagmohan, the D.D.A., the Delhi police were working on their own?

Subhadra Joshi had suggested to the people of Turkman Gate that they adopt Gandhian methods to fight Sanjay

Gandhi. She told them to stage a peaceful, sit-down *dharna* directly in front of the bulldozers, which if they moved forward would have to do so over human bodies. Thus by 8 a.m. on April 19 nearly 500 women and 200 children, wearing black armbands, squatted. Two other groups, one in front of Delite cinema, the other near Hamdard Dawakhana, also adopted similar protest techniques. These three groups constituted the forces of peaceful protest.

The forces ranged on the other side were massive. The D.D.A. officials knew confrontation was only a matter of time. As the sun rose higher (temperature: 108 degrees Farenheit) lorry-loads of police and C.R.P. started streaming in. 'They were in full battle dress—riot shields, tear-gas guns, rifles.'

The D.D.A. approached a local leader. 'We tell you once again, remove these women and children and stop holding up our work.' The leader said he was waiting for Subhadra Joshi, who had promised to come and act as mediator. 'I tell you your Mrs Joshi won't show up. She is hiding in her house. Nobody is coming to help you.'

Indeed, nobody did.

By mid-day the Delhi police were out in full force. D.I.G. Bhinder, S. P.'s Ohri and Nikhil Kumar, the sub-divisional magistrate, R. K. Patendey, plus cadres of the Nehru Brigade.

All the elements of a riot were finely poised. A restive crowd, a provocative police force, the summer heat, mutual rancour. Around 1 p.m. some of the squatters rose for their noon prayer, some, perhaps, were tired. There was movement in the crowd. In the circumstances, who chucked the first stone is an academic question, for it was inevitable that some stray spark would ignite the riot which had been brewing for many hours.

What happened next is well known. Young Abdul Malik stood up, bared his chest at the police and shouted: 'Shoot me or stop the demolition.' The police shot him. And shot others too. The firing continued till 5 in the afternoon when a curfew was imposed. It lasted forty-five days.

The stories of atrocities as enumerated by John Dayal and Ajoy Bose in their excellently researched book 'For Reasons of State: Delhi under Emergency' are strongly refuted by the Youth Congress, the D.D.A., the police and Sanjay. Dayal and Bose present first hand accounts of rape, robbery, torture. I myself heard many stories of police *zulum* in Turkman Gate, a *zulum*, which, according to the police at any rate, was in response to a three-hour 'pathroa' (stone throwing). Even if there was some stone throwing from the squatters, the police reprisal was in no way commensurate with the alleged provocation.

Casualty figures naturally vary enormously. '500 dead, hundreds missing—some of the dead were buried under the debris,' say the people of Turkman Gate. Leslie Murphy, the Reuters correspondent in India who spent almost the entire night of April 19 in Turkman Gate assessing the death count says: 'At the outside, 12 people were killed'—a figure I would be inclined to accept.

After having been mutilated, shot and killed, the uprooted people of Turkman Gate made their way to Jagmohan's resettlement colonies. 'To see the resettlement colonies through the eyes of the D.D.A. was indeed a surreal experience' say Dayal and Bose. Sanjay Gandhi boasted: 'In these colonies, about 50,000 plots, providing accommodation to about 2.5 lakh people, have been developed with all the basic, civil amenities, including pucca roads, drains, street lighting, public latrines, pure water supply, parks, playgrounds, schools, dispensaries, etc. In most of the new resettlement colonies even television and adult literacy centres have been established.'

Established? Mr Gandhi is serenely confusing his tenses. Work on the resettlement colonies began not before but after resettlement. Initially people were rounded up in trucks, taken across the Jamuna and dropped into desolation—in land that was as bald as a tennis ball. Muslim philanthropists and social workers ran a 24-hour shuttle service distributing food and medicine. At night you slept under the stars in the comforting knowledge that at least the bulldozers were far away.

Meanwhile the D.D.A. was busy constructing. One brick on top of another was termed a plot, an allotment, a house. That is the reality of operation resettlement.

A thirty minute drive from Delhi will take you to the resettlement colonies. I went in May '77 to places with names like Khichripur, Trilokpur, Kalyanipur, and there I saw the full extent of the misery perpetrated by Sanjay on these poor, defenceless people. Most of the so-called houses, even in May '77, consisted of a few bricks casually cemented together. Usually no roof existed (an intimidating prospect if you had braved one monsoon and were expecting another), mosquitoes abounded, the roads were anything but pucca. I saw no television sets.

Outside their desultory quarters, the uprooted huddled passively, motionless in their despair. Miles away from possibilities of employment, they sat resigned and despondent. (Javid Laiq, a perceptive *Indian Express* correspondent, says he saw pride and hope on the faces of these people. I did not.) What did they eat? Where was the money coming from? Why weren't they angry? The much-publicized Indian ability to survive on nothing is no foreign-journalist cliché here.

A day after the Turkman riots, a family acquaintance of the Gandhis gave an account of what 'really' happened to Rajiv and Sonia (*Samachar* had blacked out the news). 'It's none of my business,' interrupted Rajiv, while Sonia burst out: 'Why do you fill my husband's ears with poison? Why don't you leave us alone?'

Sanjay with his uncanny ability to get things wrong maintained till March 20 that the resettlement of the people of Turkman Gate was among the tallest feathers in his cap. Asked by a journalist, a week after elections had been announced, how these resettled people would vote, he said: 'I would say 95 to 99 per cent will vote in favour of Congress. Just now in Delhi I think that would be our most solid vote.'

Turkman Gate did not impede the inexorable rise of Sanjay Gandhi. For a few days he dropped out of circulation, but he was soon back. It is difficult to put a precise date, but by June '76 he was running a parallel government from inside his mother's house.

SANJAY'S DAY BEGAN AT 8 a.m. at Akbar Road. At this hour he met and briefed all those concerned with the fate of Delhi. Jagmohan, Tamta, Kishen Chand, Navin Chawla, Bhinder presented daily reports. 'They all came to take instructions from him. Most of them called him sir,' says someone who saw these early morning conferences in session. Sanjay was invariably unruffled, polite and brief to the point of being laconic. 'I never heard him shout. His orders were crystal clear and he had a very good memory. He didn't keep notes or files. Usually he never asked questions, he just listened,' says Jagdish Tytler. After having given instructions for the day—he alloted no more than that—Sanjay prepared for his next assignment.

Precisely at 8.45 a.m. Sanjay would get into his Matador and drive to the Maruti factory in Gurgaon. 'You could almost set your watch by him. He was so punctual.' He returned at 12.55 for the family luncheon, a ritual Mrs Gandhi insisted on.

In the afternoon, beginning 2 p.m., Sanjay moved to 1, Safdarjang where he busied himself in the affairs of the nation. Cabinet Ministers, Chief Ministers, Youth Congress leaders, Doon School friends all lined up. 'In any one afternoon he could have anything up to 60 appointments. He saw no one for more than five minutes.' R. K. Dhawan, who monitored the appointments, would have engagements spaced as sharply as 4.07, 4.10, 4.14. 'You would go into the room and find him seated. He would not get up or shake hands or smile. Namaste was his customary greeting.' Small talk was taboo. 'Yes?' he would say. By the time the person had made his request or complaint Sanjay had decided what course of action he would take. 'He took decisions all the time—and what he said got done.' The last engagement would be scheduled for 5.55 p.m., and at 6 Sanjay was finished for the day.

Soon his parallel government began running with such precision and got extended so vastly that the Prime Minister was squeezed out. Mrs Gandhi complained that Sanjay's visitors were taking up so much room in 1, Safdarjang that she had no place to meet her visitors.

If Sanjay was busy inside his mother's house he was even busier outside. Indeed, he seems to have undertaken a superhuman task: to wipe every tear from every face—a virtual one-man campaign to fight and defeat all national evils—in six months.

'He saved millions of pensioners who had to run from pillar to post to get their dues by prompt intervention.' He nursed the sick in missionary charities, presenting cheques. He flew into Madras to solace and cheer 'the flood-hit people,' and made arrangements for the accomodation of over 7,000 people. When asked how he would like to celebrate his birthday, he said: 'How will it profit anybody to celebrate my birthday? Go to the poorest and weakest among the people and provide them with a day they would like to celebrate—that is the kind of birthday gift I would like to have'—subsequently the D.S.I.D.C. 'decided to give Sanjay a birthday gift which even Gandhiji would envy' (Sanjay laid the foundation stone of a labour colony for 500 workers). He offered *bidi* and salt to the tribals of Raipur. He inaugurated a Rs 80 crore irrigation scheme in Patna. He opened a game sanctuary. He launched a programme of 'debt redemption which would benefit 31,000 persons'. He joined volunteers in Shramdan to build roads. He 'saved' the Taj in Agra by quashing 'silly ideas of opening a bar' next to the monument. He donated his eyes posthumously.

It was an incredible performance, a tribute to Sanjay's indefatigable energy and a tribute to high class humbug.

Both critics and admirers of Sanjay are agreed that Gauhati was the summit of his short though tumultuous political career.

Jawahar Nagar, Gauhati, was earmarked as the arena of the 1976 annual convention of the Congress Party. The dates fixed were 21 and 22 November. Significantly, the Youth Congress was scheduled to have its 'first annual convention', also at Jawahar Nagar two days earlier—on 19 and 20 November.

Meticulous preparations had been made to take the wind out of the second convention. Invitations to 92 countries were despatched asking them to send youth representatives. Finally only 29 countries accepted the invitation, and only 60 foreign delegates turned up. 'Many western countries excused themselves on the ground that they had no youth organizations.'

'Gauhati goes gay' chorused the newspaper headlines. For the over 30s the experience was less gay. The whole city seemed to be in the throes of some primitive fever. Banners, festoons, bunting, arches 'decorated the city'. A phantom 'tent city', Yuva Nagar, sprouted overnight, plastered with placards and posters heralding the rise of the Youth Congress under Sanjay. One poster said, 'Sanjay Gandhi, you are the helmsman of our new India, the country's last resort'. Another stated: 'Welcome future light of India'.

President Ambika Soni, her four general secretaries and all the National Committee members stayed in the tent city. It seems Sanjay was keen to pitch in too, but for security reasons he moved in with his mother at a 'newly constructed guest house'.

Sanjay's entry into Gauhati was appropriately 'ecstatic.' The 30-kilometre route from Boryor airport to Yuva Nagar 'was lined by thousands of people. A helicopter with a bright young lady, Kalpana Misra, showered confetti... Young boys and girls danced with joy at the fulfilment of their dream ... Sanjay was taken in a procession flanked by horse riders and motorcycle outriders. He stood throughout the route, waving at thousands of men, women and children who cheered him and greeted him with claps. It appeared as if the entire 2 lakh population of the city had come to see him... the city had not seen a sight like that in recent years.'

The opening of the first Youth Congress convention was timed to coincide with Indira Gandhi's birthday. The real purpose of the convention, however, was anything but festive. Sanjay and his brigade had arrived with definite plans. They were going to ridicule, mock, terrorize, and finally take over the Party. This coup d'etat wasn't left to chance. Before he came to the convention, Sanjay had decided to carry the fight into the enemy's camp—for despite all the provocation in the past, Congress leaders had refused to pick up his gauntlet. (The number of delegates attending is a matter of debate. Figures from 15,000 to 50,000 are mentioned. The *New York Times* man, Bill Borders, detected only 6,000. Independent observers confirm that they saw around 10,000 young men and women on the opening day.)

The pace-setter of the convention was Ambika Soni. She made sure the Congress President was on stage when she thanked him for his cooperation. But she regretted that that cooperation had been stinting, reluctant. 'She lashed out at the Congressmen who were obstructing the constructive programme of the Youth Congress... She complained that the Youth Congress workers at the district and block level faced difficulties in implementing the 5-point programme.' Making a frontal charge and pointing an accusing finger at Barooah she warned: 'I want to bring it to your notice—Congressmen obstruct the work of the Youth Congress. They fear that the Youth Congress may take the lead in their areas by hard work. We are not hungry for power, but we will fight back if you people continue to obstruct us'.

Head bowed, Barooah listened as the thousands of delegates gave Mrs Soni 'a standing ovation'. Just before Ambika sat down she performed her real role. She clutched the mike, and shouted: 'Sanjay Gandhi Zindabad' three times. The audience chipped in three times.

It was Sanjay's turn next, and for once he made a half-way decent crack. 'A year ago the Congress held its session in Chandigarh while the Youth Congress held a cell meeting. This year the Youth Congress is holding its session while the Congress will hold a small cell meeting.' If the press is to be believed 'rhythmic applause' ensued and 'Sanjay had to pause for some time before he could return to his speech.'

The incitement to revolt was now total. Sanjay suggested to his young followers not to seek assistance or help from state governments or pradesh congress committees. 'They only want to hold you back.' He continued: 'What do we want? If we wish to remain *chelas* and *chamchas* of others let us continue to take their help and follow them as their tail. But if you want the Youth Congress to be a work-oriented organization determined to shape the future of India, then we can't follow someone holding his tail.'

Perhaps the most insulting quip of the day came not from Ambika or Sanjay but from a relatively junior luminary of the M.P. Youth Congress, Mahesh Joshi. He said: 'What is the use of going to Mr Barooah for anything. He is sleeping most of the time.'

The big event of the next day was the valedictory address by the Prime Minister. There had been some speculation that Mrs Gandhi might cool the heat and work toward a rapprochement between the warring factions of her party. Instead she added a few sparks of her own. Applauding her son's 5-point programme she said it was complementary to her own. Then came the immortal passage: 'You have stolen our thunder, and it should be that way. I have firm faith in the youth of India.

If they can look after this country then India's future is safe.' That was just the kind of endorsement Sanjay was looking for. Mrs Gandhi stood shoulder-to-shoulder with him and the Youth Congress.

When all the clapping and cheering had died down—it continued in the press for some weeks—two things emerged.

Around November '76 Mrs Gandhi was finally sold on dynastic succession, not only on grounds of filial devotion but because she thought the country's destiny safe in her son's hands. Sanjay would gradually take over the running of government while she would gradually recede into the background. I am not sure if Mrs Gandhi had any great plans for the Youth Congress; she was hoping, as was Sanjay, that it would provide a springboard for her son to leap from youth to national fame. No coincidence then that in December '76 the Censors issued a written directive to the press asking it to refrain from using the prefix 'youth leader' in connection with Mr Sanjay Gandhi. When a reporter in Bombay asked Sanjay why he had suddenly taken a dislike to the title 'youth leader', Sanjay replied: 'It was very stupid.'

The second thing to emerge from Gauhati, in retrospect, of course, was that Sanjay and the Youth Congress had overplayed their hand. The open show of hostility had antoganized not only the Left wing of the party but the Centre and the Right. The prospect of hordes of gruff young men and women seizing the party structure from the grassroots upwards seemed imminent. Congressmen now were not fighting for ideology or personal gain, they were fighting for survival.

One other political party was concerned about its future—the C.P.I. At every opportunity Sanjay got, he 'blasted' the Communists.. He accused them of being corrupt, of being on the pay roll of Moscow, of treason. (Sanjay resurrected the Communist Party's refusal to support Gandhi's 1942 Quit India call). Earlier he had come down heavily on the pro-C.P.I. daily *Patriot*, which while being pathetically servile to Mrs Gandhi refused to recognise her son. Mohammad Yunus, a grotesque, crude and vulgar Sanjay goon who seems to have got off lightly, cancelled all government advertising to the paper. How *Patriot* survived the Emergency is a minor miracle.

The prevailing attitude to the C.P.I. was best summed up by Ayub Syed, editor of *Current*: 'The emergence of the Youth Congress as a militant force dedicated to the reconstruction of the country has unnerved the ageing, opportunistic and intellectually dishonest leaders of the Communist Party of India. They are unable to stomach a rejuvenated young India with Sanjay Gandhi as its charismatic leader'.

The C.P.I. indeed could not stomach Sanjay. They had been quietly but consistently sniping at him since the Emergency. They could hardly do otherwise with Sanjay publicly damning and threatening to destroy them.

It was the C.P.I. which first spotted the existence of a caucus—so familiar later on—and referred to it in print. The General Secretary of the C.P.I., Rajeshwar Rao, alleged: 'The caucus inside the ruling party has a comprehensive plan to borrow the central administration, remove chief ministers not prepared to act according to their will, have liaison with reaction outside, capture power and replace the present parliamentary set up...' But the real target of C.P.I, wrath, even more than the caucus, was Sanjay Gandhi's 5-point Youth Congress plan. Mohit Sen, a noted communist idealogue, saw parallels between the Youth Congress in India and the fascist youths of Nazi Germany. 'Orders', wrote Mr Sen in the

Party paper *New Age*, 'are issued by a coterie and all that the others have to do is to instantly and obediently implement these orders'.

The most urbane criticism came from the serene and civilized editor of *Mainstream*, Nikhil Chakrovarti. He saw consistency in Mrs Gandhi's you've-stolen-our-thunder speech in Gauhati. 'She was not indulging in hyperbole but announcing the carefully planned enthronement of a new element in national politics... From the curiosity piece going up in a gas balloon at Chandigarh, Sanjay Gandhi has been marked out at Gauhati to be installed as the Number Two, next only to his mother ... Gauhati saw the annointing of the Prince of Wales of Indian politics...' Only a brave man would express himself thus in December '76.

In a startling, rambling, bitter, 100-minute speech, Mrs Gandhi spiritedly came to her son's defence and attacked her electoral allies by name—something she had not done since 1969. 'They (C.P.I.) say they support me; but there can be no greater insult than to say that I could be influenced by reactionaries or anybody else. If I am a person who is so influenced I have no business to be Prime Minister of India.'

Mrs Gandhi then went on to make an extraordinary claim. 'Sanjay is much too small a fry. Obviously he is not going to be the prime minister or the president or anything like this. All he can be is a Congress worker. Therefore the attack on him is very definitely on me.' Mother and son had been emotionally inseparable, now they were politically inseparable.

Sanjay had been gunning for what he called 'communist infiltrators' into the Congress—the traditional left, fellow-travellers, card-carrying members who had mellowed. Prominent in his list of wanted men and women were Nandini

Satpathy, Siddharth Shankar Ray, Dev Kant Barooah, Rajni Patel, Chandrajit Yadav. All these people had at various times tried 'to fall in line' with Sanjay but he refused to accept them in its camp.

Nandini Satpathy went down gloriously. Perhaps she 'didn't play her cards too well,' however, she was the first Congress leader to challenge Sanjay's extra-constitutional authority. Alas, she tried to build up her own son as some kind of youth leader, and he, to compound matters, set up a parallel youth party in Orissa. Nandini stood up bravely to a barrage of sustained press abuse and villification—'tame empress of Orissa', 'Nandini bares fangs', 'Smash Orissa commies'—and she only withdrew when Kamlapathi Tripathi rang her up on behalf of Mrs Gandhi and told her that the choice was between dismissal and resignation.

Mr Rajni Patel made every effort to placate Sanjay Gandhi. Rajni's final attempt was in early November when he invited Mr Gandhi to Bombay and provided him with 'an unforgettable welcome.' Sanjay arrived with his wife, and in his first public engagement in the city lashed out at the person who had invited him. The B.P.C.C., (of which Rajni Patel was the President and presiding god) observed Mr Gandhi, 'has betrayed the trust of the people', it's only purpose seemed to be money collection. 'You should serve the people', chastised Sanjay. Subsequently Mr Patel's name was seen less frequently in the press, he did not go to Gauhati, and in early January '76 he resigned, unmourned and unlamented.

In terms of hierarchy and stature Siddarth Shanker Ray was senior to both Nandini and Rajni Patel. Mr Ray enjoyed a personal relationship — he called her 'Indu' — with Mrs Gandhi which was the envy of other Congress leaders, and he was the only chief minister to have a direct telephone link with the Prime Minister.

Like Nandini, Siddharth fought gamely—and won. In November '76 when Mr Gandhi was taking 'West Bengal by storm', Siddharth and Sanjay spoke from a common platform in Calcutta without mentioning each other by name. Moreover, Mr Ray was in the habit of not being present at the airport when the Youth Congress leader arrived. Indeed, he had urged fellow chief ministers to follow his example. Thus, while Mr Gandhi demanded subservience, Mr Ray 'spoke only to the P.M.'

By December '76 Sanjay had the West Bengal chief boxed in. Two important portfolios were taken from him and given to those ministers who had been encouraged to agitate for his removal. To aggravate matters Sanjay thrust his Doon School buddy, Kamal Nath, into West Bengal politics, and the latter began meddling in Youth Congress affairs. This was too much provocation for Das Munshi, and for starters he burned Mr Kamal Nath's car to ashes. Munshi also quickly patched up a long-standing feud with Ray, and together they presented a joint front to Sanjay.

The Centre's criticism of Ray and his administration was along familiar lines. Ray had failed to provide leadership, the state was falling behind, the 25-point plan was being inefficiently implemented, corruption was rampant, the law and order situation was grave. Although Ray refuted all these allegations, he was very much on the defensive.

With Munshi by his side, Ray moved from defence to offence. Banking on Bengali chauvinism, he cleverly turned his own struggle for survival into a state-centre struggle. What was at stake, he implied, was the dignity and pride of West Bengal.

Could the state allow itself to be dictated by the whims and caprices of New Delhi?

No great resistance was forthcoming from Barooah and Yadav, perhaps because they were political light-weights. Sanjay disliked the Congress President more than Yadav, not so much for the ideology he represented but for his physical appearance. 'That buffoon,' was how Sanjay saw Mr Barooah.

Actually, Mr Gandhi was not the only Youth Congress leader to nourish ministerial ambitions. Ambika Soni, too, saw herself as cabinet minister material. She had, of course, abandoned her earlier hopes of manipulating and dominating Sanjay, and accepted the role of the loyal lieutenant—something she seemed to do, publicly at least, with exemplary servitude.

After Gauhati, however, there were persistent leaks in the press about Mrs Soni's impending retirement. One began to hear and see Ambika decreasingly on the media—a sure sign of political banishment those days. Mrs Soni complains of vested interests who sabotaged her relationship with Sanjay, while Jagdish Tytler maintains that Ambika suffered due to her own network of spies and informers and due to her overriding political aspirations. Tytler also accuses Mrs Soni of embezzling Youth Congress funds.

By the fag end of '76 Mrs Soni was out of favour. She was no longer seen by Sanjay's side on his tours, as chief ministers and local Youth Congress leaders only invited Mr Gandhi. In fact, they made sure that Mrs Soni remained uninvited.

Why the discourtesy? Even in her role of loyal lieutenant Mrs Soni had become a threat to Sanjay. 'She cut a better figure on public platforms', she was attractive and intelligent, on radio and TV she came across persuasively, foreign journalists found her 'smart, receptive and good company'. Altogether her media abilities were 'streets ahead of Sanjay'—a situation which greatly disturbed the Sanjay sellers. It is no coincidence I think, that after Gauhati the media found less and less time for the President of the Youth Congress. Mrs Soni was in fact being 'played down'.

While Sanjay Gandhi was enjoying and consolidating his transition from youth to national leader, Mrs Gandhi was contemplating the most controversial, baffling and ultimately, disastrous, decision of her political career. Historians, biographers, social analysts will no doubt argue endlessly about Indira's 'matter of faith' as declared to the people of India on 18 January 1977. To date, however, none of the reasons forwarded for 'going to the country' seem entirely satisfactory. Duped by intelligence agencies, convinced of victory, bowing to international pressure, reacting to Bhutto, cut off from reality, 'really had faith in democratic institutions'—these are the explanations offered.

While these considerations played some part in the final decision, I think we should consider one more factor: instinct. Mrs Gandhi's major political victories have all been as much the result of sagacity and intrigue as they have been of timing. I don't know where Indira inherited her built-in timing radar which enabled her in the past to strike with such devastating precision. What failed in 1977, as far as she was concerned, was not the Emergency, but this radar. As a politician she lived by instinct and died by instinct.

Some people are convinced that Sanjay is at heart a totalitarian, that he has no faith in the democratic process. I have no hard evidence to substantiate that belief but if one goes by Mr Gandhi's previous spoken record, then that view is hard to refute. At any rate he did not consider the periodic renewal of mandate as the life blood of democracy. What was infinitely more important to him was 'development', and since India was developing so rapidly under the Emergency, why upset the 'rate of growth'. He said in December '76: 'Future generations will not remember us by how many elections we had, but by the progress we have made'. The only problem with this approach to progress is that Emergency tends to become permanent, because you find your 'rate of growth' has mysteriously disappeared as soon as civic freedoms are restored. Sanjay, in my view, had no congenital antipathy to democracy; he just thought it irrelevant.

If Sanjay had, as most people believe, a complete hold over his mother, why did he permit her to announce elections? I can't pretend I know the answer to that riddle; I do know that after the Congress defeat, when someone asked Sanjay why he sat idly by and watched his mother destroy herself, he said: 'I couldn't help it. She was too much influenced by the communists'—which, if nothing else, proves that Mr Gandhi consistently opposed the January poll, although he publicly made the right noises.

Once elections were called, the immediate reaction was: she's done it again. The timing was thought to be perfect, what with the gains of the Emergency, the Opposition in disarray and so little time for her opponents to mount an effective campaign. The Youth Congress, sensing their moment of triumph, moved in for the kill. 'For the first time in democratic India,' wrote Ayub Syed, 'elections will be organized, dominated, fought and won by the Youth Congress under the leadership of Sanjay Gandhi.' The expected Youth Congress cry went out: 200 seats! Considering the prevailing mood, that seemed like a modest demand!

Only till February 2. Then Mr Jagjivan Ram exploded his 'J-bomb' and shot down Sanjay's soaring kite. Finally the Youth Congress secured less than ten nominations—and on March 21 lost them all.

Indiri Bachao[1]

(save your penis)

EVERY SEVENTH PERSON IN the world is an Indian; and by 2001, if the current rate of population upsurge continues, every sixth person will be an Indian.

Newly born children are a recent problem for India. Till 1921 natural forces—epidemics, famine, drought, flood, malnutrition—created a finely balanced holding line: the born roughly equalled the dead. So that in 1922 the birth rate per 1,000 of the population was 48.1 and the death rate was 47.2. The ensuing growth rate of .9 per 1000 was comfortably absorbed.

By 1931 the situation was less happy. The triple benefits of modern medicine, improved hygiene and better diet wiped

1 This was the cry heard in villages all over north India during the Emergency.

out nature's ecological balance. While the birth rate remained 48.1, the death rate dropped to 36.3 per 1,000. In only ten years the population shot up by 28 million.

And from '31 onwards the population chart never stood still, instead it deteriorated rapidly as the gap between birth and death rates continued to widen. In 1951 while the birth rate remained constant the death rate had fallen to 27.4, and in 1961 to 22.8 per 1,000.

Ideally, a family planning programme, even a tentative one, should have been launched in the 30s when it became apparent that India would produce more mouths than it could feed. But the British were more concerned with consolidating their own kingdom rather than worrying about mounting hungry native mouths. The raj was minority, white and desperately in need of English babies. Colonial logic saw no need for family planning for the rulers or the ruled.

Expectedly, the population graph continued its relentless upward spiral. The birth rate in 1971 was 39.0 per 1,000 while the death rate was as low as 17.4.

By 1973 the statistics were as unambiguous as they were alarming. India was adding to its population over 12 million people annually[2]—and this in a way was the good news, for a projection based on this rate of increase predicted a population double by the end of the century. The daunting prospect of a billion bodies jostling for survival looms on the horizon today.

The extraordinary aspect of this frightening situation is that government, bureaucracy, intelligentsia, even ordinary middle class people, are aware of the enormity of the problem facing

2 The figure stands at 14 million today.

the nation. In fact, mouthing the value of planned parenthood has become something of a truism today.

For years now editorials have been written, seminars held, ministerial speeches made, international conferences hosted, White Papers issued emphasizing the do-or-die urgency of a speedy, well-orchestrated family planning programme in India. Incredibly, figures bandied around in an effort to shock and jolt only serve to bore or amuse: India acquires each year the total population of Australia; 60,000 babies are born every day; the number of people living in Bombay city are more than the number of people living in Norway; if Indians stood shoulder to shoulder in a single line it would stretch from Lucknow to Luxembourg... and so on.

A French economist returning home after a three-month tour of India expressed his exasperation thus: 'I can't explain how amazed I am at the casualness with which the single greatest menace facing India is being tackled. It is so dangerous to give family planning the low priority it has here. The problem is so obvious, its manifestations so stark. What amazes me even further is that all the senior government officials I have met seem to be aware of the hazards of unchecked population growth. Yet I can see no co-ordinated programme.'

The French economist wasn't being entirely fair.

When the first Health Minister of India, Rajkumari Amrit Kaur, took office, India's population stood at 320 million. She vaguely recognized the need 'to do something' about overpopulation and added a family planning department to her ministry. She even invited a U.S. specialist, Dr Abraham Stone, the inventor of the 'rhythm' method, to propagate his contraceptive in India.

A small target village was selected for 'operation rhythm'. Coloured bead necklaces were issued to the women with instructions that green beads meant 'safe' while red beads meant 'dangerous'. All the women had to do was to keep a watch on the beads and move one daily. On the face of it, a simple, safe method, tailor-made for unsophisticated village women. But, as Ashish Bose, an economist supervising the scheme found out, it had indigenous complications. 'The necklaces were of no value, so the women didn't want to wear them. They would give them to their children as toys. The children, of course, would shift all the beads around. Out of every 100 women who received the necklaces, 50 became pregnant.'

Dom Moraes in his book *A Matter of People* records another method employed by the government. 'In the late 60s an elephant was acquired whose function was to amble around the rural areas near Delhi carrying condoms, which it distributed free, to the supposedly eager populace ... I saw the animal in action: it clearly preferred children to adults and scattered its cargo freely amidst the toddlers of every village it visited. The toddlers instantly saw the practical value of the rubbers, blew them up into small balloons and tied them to sticks. A slogan in family planning is that your children should be happy. In that sense I suppose the campaign succeeded—these children most certainly were.'

Comedy went further. Certain states offered free transistors as a sterilization incentive. It seemed a wise and seductive bait since by the early 60s the transistor was an established status-symbol. People duly lined up for the operation and the states suddenly discovered that they had grossly underestimated demand. There was a shortage of transistors! Frantic calls were made to Japan in an effort to procure more sets. However, while the negotiations were in progress, the Reserve Bank refused to sanction the required foreign exchange!

In the 70s family planning acquired a hint of seriousness—but nothing else. Indeed, even a charitable assessment of the programme since Independence must warrant the conclusion that it has been unimaginative, half-hearted, inefficient and, finally, dishonest. Successive Congress governments were satisfied that each Five Year Plan alloted sums for birth control and that these sums were consumed. No one bothered to investigate if public money was being efficaciously spent. Indeed, as most people knew, it was not.

There was good reason for this indifference. Politicians in India, like politicians all over the world, are dedicated to survival, and they knew that family planning seriously pursued would be electorally disastrous. Firstly, it would offend deep and fundamental social and spiritual values of the majority of the voters; secondly, it would produce no quick 'gains'—a programme of this kind being by its very nature of long-term impact.

MR SASTI BRATA HAS not said many intelligent things in his life. In May '77, however, he did make a thoughtful observation. 'The elections,' he declared, 'have not proved that democracy flourishes in India; the elections have only proved that men don't like to lie on tables and have their things cut off.'

Not many Indians would dispute that observation. The dreaded nasbandi (sterilization)—or in Mr Brata's felicitious phrase 'things cut off'—struck demonic terror in the north and precipitated Mrs Gandhi's ignominious defeat.

Sanjay didn't know much about family planning before the

Emergency and he knew even less about nasbandi. No one had heard him express any views on the subject, and even in Uma Vasudev's in-depth Emergency interview, which marked Sanjay's entry into public life, there is no mention of the population explosion or methods to contain it. Obviously, he was in this, as in other areas, a learner.

He was, however, looking, and looking desperately, for a specific major national ailment which he could spectacularly remedy. Planting trees, eradicating dowry, cleaning lanes, promoting literacy was all very well, but it was hardly the stuff to build charismatic leadership credentials on.

Family planning was. Here was a herculean project, the solving of which, everyone acknowledged, was vital if the nation hoped to survive, much less prosper. All the benefits of the green revolution, the technological breakthrough, the export achievement, the buffer food stock were pitifully inadequate in a country whose population galloped away. If Sanjay could even minimally arrest this acceleration it would be a stupendous achievement calling for national and international acclaim.

Thus family planning became the lynch pin of Sanjay Gandhi's Emergency activities. And he himself became totally identified with it. True, he was involved in other aspects of 'nation building' and 'national cleaning', but it was on family planning that he rested his political fortunes, hoping to succeed where so many others had so manifestly failed.

Even before 25 June 1975, Mrs Gandhi was under pressure from the major western industrial democracies, speaking through the International Monetary Fund (I.M.F.) and the World Bank and the Aid-India Consortium to impart a sense of 'urgency' and 'realism' to the family planning programme in India. There was talk of launching a crash programme on a 'war footing', not to replace but to complement the one already in existence.

It would be well to remember that the I.M.F., World Bank and Aid-India are essentially lending and borrowing organizations. More sophisticated than the rapacious village money-lender, their aims are roughly equivalent: to ensure safe returns. Periodically, they publicly go through the motions of professing faith in the capacity of developing and Third World countries to achieve a degree of 'stabilisation', a balance between production and consumption. Privately, they are convinced that most of these countries, with their weak and corrupt democratic institutions (ideally they would like to do business with non-communist dictatorships and juntas), are variations of 'basket cases'.[3] The rich western nations pay lip-service to edifying slogans like 'new economic order', 'equitable distribution of world wealth' not out of a sense of guilt or fair play but because of raw material location. In reality their main concern is to curb population escalation in Asia, Africa and parts of South America. Having basket cases is bad enough, having continuously bigger baskets would be intolerable.

Consequently the I.M.F., World Bank, Aid-India axis had been quietly but firmly advocating a crash sterilization based family planning programme—crash because, according to them, valuable time had been squandered since 1947.

If their motives could be faulted their choice of contraceptive could not. The condom had been tried, the loop had been tried, the diaphragm had been tried, the rhythm method had been

---

3 'A basket case'—that's how Mr Kissinger described Bangladesh.

tried, even the pill had had limited circulation. Collectively and separately these birth control devices had failed to make any measurable impact; at best their efficacy was 40 to 60 per cent.

More than efficacy these methods were intrinsically unsuitable in the kind of social conditions which prevailed in India. 'The difficulties of a village couple who want to practice birth control are real. And they are physical as well as mental … most joint families sleep in a sort of communal bedroom. There is little space in which to store anything, and it is impossible to keep what you possess a secret from the rest of the family. Hence supplies of condoms and oral contraceptives are soon discovered by the elders who are bound to disapprove. Moreover, the difficulties of arising at night in an unlit or crowded room to find a condom are considerable. The same applies to the diaphragm … The best opportunity for sexual activity is in the fields where it often occurs spontaneously, and neither husband nor wife, however much they may want to practice family planning, has had any chance of preparing for it.'

In such social circumstances, sterilization was the only answer.

Once the Emergency had been imposed, the western-backed lobby began selling the sterilization programme with even greater vigour—and Mrs Gandhi bought it. She had to do something 'so that people would forget the court case'.[4]

Her advisers were less enthusiastic (they complained that 'the westerners had Mrs Gandhi's ears'). Mr C.H. Hanumantha Rao was of the opinion that 'the increase in population in rural

---

4 Yunus, Mohd.

areas contributed to agricultural growth'. P.N. Dhar felt the emphasis should be on economic development rather than birth control. The Union Health Minister, Karan Singh, had frequently stated that in India 'the best contraceptive is economic development'. Even the loyal Mohammad Yunus had some reservations: he felt—and how right he was—the Muslims would fight nasbandi.

As one would expect, the western lobby won the argument. Mrs Gandhi was persuaded to incorporate sterilization into her Emergency package, and she handed over the responsibility of execution to her son. Sanjay, for reasons discussed earlier, accepted the task gleefully.

Sterilization, no doubt, was *the* birth control panacea for India. The surgery involved was minor: it lasted no more than three minutes, could be performed on local anaesthesia, needed no hospitalization, and in the words of Dr Pai, a devoted and tireless apostle of sterilization, 'without a drop of blood'.

But it did involve an operation whereas the loop, diaphragm, *nirodh* did not. In India where there was resistance to conventional contraception (the arguments are only too familiar: one mouth equals two hands, old age security, continuation of family tree, joy of parenthood) a birth control method which required 'cutting up insides' was bound to meet furious hostility.

To begin with, there were pervasive myths associated with the operation, the most potent of which concerned virility. It was rumoured that once a vasectomy or tubectomy was performed, the person lost interest in sex. Worse, and this was true for men, one became impotent! In a country where being 'a man', where the ability to impregnate one's wife was almost as sacred as one's honour, the impotency myth turned out to be the single biggest obstacle to sterilization.

There were other myths also: you were supposed to become 'like a stick' after the operation, you couldn't work because of tiredness,[5] your wife would become promiscuous (wives were not supposed to have similar fears about their husbands), you would die on the operating table, your vital organs would become infected.

None of these myths were scientifically or biologically valid. However, vasectomies and tubectomies were not a matter of science and biology alone, they touched on dark regions of the psyche. The mind and the spirit were the nesting ground of these myths and before any national sterilization programme could be effectively launched they would have to be neutralized.

Myths, after all, are nothing but a product of prejudice and ignorance. And in the case of sterilization it was certainly possible, with gentle tact and sustained persuasion, to prove that these myths were nothing but in fact prejudice and ignorance. (It may be pertinent to record here that Indians are not alone in harbouring irrational sterilization fears. In Italy, Spain and South America there has been even greater resistance to this method of family planning, based, interestingly, on the same kind of fears.)

The problem, of course, was that Sanjay did not have the time for gentle tact and sustained persuasion. He wanted results, latest by day after tomorrow. A young man in a hurry,

---

5 The men also had to put up with ridicule. A 40-year-old villager complained: 'The women tell us we are not men any more and that we should work in the kitchen.'

he disastrously miscalculated the quantum of 'motivation' necessary to get people to the operating table. He consulted nobody in the Ministry of Health, and even if he had it is doubtful if anyone would have had the courage to tell him that the kind of sterilization programme he envisaged would require at least two years of continuous education and instruction before it could get off the ground. Karan Singh knew this, but he was a dummy minister anyway.

Even though he was in a hurry, Sanjay had to wait some months before he could launch his programme. The mechanics had to be defined, key men and women had to be selected to execute, some flimsy infrastructure had to be built. In Delhi (the programme was first briefly test marketed in the capital before it was nationally launched, and it succeeded only in those states which had Sanjay-approved chief ministers) the responsibility for this was mainly given to four people: The Lt. Governor, Kishen Chand, Navin Chawla, Vidyaben Shah and Rukhsana Sultana.

There was, at least in Delhi, some token gesture towards education and persuasion. On 25 December 1975 Vidyaben Shah met Kishen Chand and a 'Family Planning Motivation Committee' was convened. About the same time, Rukhsana Sultana, whose previous occupation was that of a boutique owner, went up to Sanjay Gandhi, introduced herself and asked: 'What can *I* do for you?' Sanjay replied: 'You are a Muslim, go into the walled city.' Among Rukhsana's chief tasks there was sterilization motivation. Sanjay was determined that his programme begin in the walled city of old Delhi, which, as everyone knows, is predominantly inhabited by Muslims.

Of all the communities in India, the Muslims had—or so they thought—most to fear from family planning. A minority among a huge majority, they felt there was safety only in numbers. To them all talk of population control was a Hindu plot whose only purpose was to achieve their gradual extinction.

Would it have been better then, to start a sterilization programme in a more secularly populated area rather than in old Delhi? Sanjay didn't think so. He believed if he could break resistance in a Muslim stronghold like old Delhi he would have no problem elsewhere. (Some people have attributed communal motives to Sanjay's choice of site. I found no evidence to support that interpretation.) It was this logic that carried sterilization, as it were, into the lion's den.

Vidyaben Shah held durbars on the steps of Jama Masjid propagating the boons of vasectomies and tubectomies, while Rukhsana, taking advantage of her faith, went into *purdah* houses spreading the same message.

The audience reaction and response was not altogether un-encouraging. The women seemed particularly receptive. Most of them had had six to eight children of which, if they were lucky, half had survived. Rukhsana remembers asking one woman how many children she had. The woman thought for five seconds, began counting on her fingers and replied, 'eleven—no, no, twelve'.

There was a genuine desire for information. Was the operation safe? How long would it take? Could it be reversed? And then hesistantly, softly, 'Would it diminish virility?'

Both Rukhsana and Vidyaben Shah's Committee had no experience at answering these kind of questions. They had no social work background, no printed literature, no charts; they didn't take along a nurse or doctor who could have answered the medical queries authoritatively. Rukhsana herself confesses 'she was embarrassed' talking about the operation. It is a wonder that such ill-qualified motivators had any audience at all.

Nevertheless, the Muslim women and men of old Delhi were listening. If you were not sure of your next meal and had eight children, not having any more made very real sense. A little time, some patience, more prodding and most of the people would have come to the operating table of their own free will.

In early March, the sterilization camps had begun functioning in Delhi. On the first day nineteen volunteers turned up, the next day no one turned up, and the next day saw three people in queue. Already the rumours were in circulation, and already some of the methods of 'motivation', which were to become characteristic later on, were in evidence. Navin Chawla wasn't depressed by the scarcity in numbers. 'It's a time consuming process,' he said, 'it needs constant vigilance so that such rumours don't spread.'

The 'such rumours' Mr Chawla glossed over were about compulsion and coercion. Word had spread that intimidation, threat, blackmail and force was to be used to obtain 'volunteers'. Free will, which was supposed to be the basis of the programme, was a façade.

As much as Sanjay tried, the programme wouldn't take off. It lacked momentum and thrust and direction. Sanjay had officially blessed the camps and each morning Kishen Chand and Chawla provided him with progress reports. The count of 25 or 30 or 35 per day didn't please him at all. Kishen Chand wanted more funds and more volunteers, but neither man-power nor money were able to raise the count. On March 24, forty operations were performed—and that was a record!

The police till now had been rounding up with a measure of restraint; 75 rupees, a week off work, a tin of ghee ensured, with proper guidance, two or three dozen sweepers, rickshawalas and labourers.

This, however, was not the kind of figure Sanjay had in mind. Desperate, he called in the D.I.G. of Police, Bhinder and ordered him to get more 'volunteers', how he got them was his business. 'One had to prevent,' said Chawla, 'poor people living like animals and breeding more poor people.'

Bhinder was given a completely free hand and police quotas were fixed for each camp.

Sanjay himself stepped into the open. Addressing a youth rally in Delhi he said, 'Some so called leaders within and without the Congress are opposing the family planning programme… Any leader of any community or religion who opposes family planning should not be accepted as a leader… They should be thrown out.'

In one speech Sanjay silenced two sets of critics. One was the old guard Congress which had been covertly attacking the programme because they feared it would be unpopular at the grassroots level. The second was the religious leaders for whom sterilization, indeed family planning, was contrary to holy scriptures. Not surprisingly the Chief Censor of India issued a dictat to the press on April 1: 'No criticism of the family planning programme. This includes letters to the editor.'

To further strengthen Sanjay's hand, the Government announced on April 16 a National Population Policy Statement which clearly stated that sterilization would be the main plank of family planning in India. A target figure of 4 million was announced for the year with the long term objective of reducing the birth rate from 3.4 per cent to 1.4 per cent by the early 1980s.

With no fear of press or party censure, Kishen Chand and the police set about their task vigorously. And almost overnight there was an amazing spurt in the figures. Even Sanjay didn't expect such results so quickly. The daily count in May for Delhi alone went up from 30 to 300, and in June to 700.

By June the programme was also in full swing in the states, notably U.P., M.P., Rajasthan, Bihar, Orissa, Haryana, Punjab, Himachal Pradesh—an area which after the elections came to be known as the 'vasectomy belt.' The Chief Ministers were responsible for implementing the programme in their states and they too used Delhi's motivational methods. Where previously the daily national count for tubectomies and vasectomies was 331, it shot up in one month to 1,578, and by August it was 5,644.

Delhi, naturally, was tops. *Current,* the Sanjay Gandhi mouthpiece, stated: 'Delhi tops all states in family planning with 41.3 per cent couples covered by the scheme as against a national average of 16.1 per cent.' Was there any compulsion? 'If there was any coercion,' said Vidyaben Shah, 'the job would have been finished overnight. The very fact that we have been spending *so much time* (italics mine) in order to convince people shows that there is no coercion.'

Sanjay was continuously exhorting his people for better and better results. He had every reason to. Things were going not only according to plan, but way beyond plan. Why, he argued, couldn't they go even further. For example, by incessantly pushing Kishen Chand and Chawla in Delhi he had achieved 1,67,000 sterilizations in just 167 days—a figure that was equal to the total for the last ten years.

When chief ministers came to visit him, as was their wont, he would point out the spectacular record of Delhi. The chief ministers would go back to their respective states and up their quotas. Or alternately he would run chief minister against chief minister. When Hardeo Joshi came to meet Sanjay, Sanjay spoke to him glowingly about the excellent work done by S. C. Shukla in Madhya Pradesh. '600,000 operations in two weeks,' he told Joshi. Joshi hung down his head in shame, rushed back to Jaipur and ordered acceleration at all camps in his state. Soon, he too had excellent results to report—1,24,500 sterilizations in one month when the annual target for Rajasthan was 1,75,000.

'Figures for vasectomy and tubectomy operations have become something of a national game. States and the various regions within states have been encouraged to vie with each other in performance,' reported Reuters in a dispatch from Delhi.

Meanwhile, *Samachar* was assiduously promoting an impression of peace, happiness and tranquility. People throughout the length and breadth of the country were voluntarily flocking to operating tables and saluting Sanjay Gandhi for the magnificent programme he had initiated! A Delhi municipal worker, it seemed, cycled eight kilometers for his operation. When he was given his incentive money, he added a rupee from his own pocket and handed the money back. 'Family planning is a national task. This is my humble contribution,' he announced. Another man from Ratnagiri said 'Enough is enough' as he walked into a clinic. He had 38 children and had at last seen the light. In Bhopal, Islam Ahmed was garlanded, cheered and taken round the city on horseback: After four wives and nineteen children he'd been 'motivated'.

There was good news from foreign countries too. An Australian doctor after studying 50 sterilized couples for six months reported 'greater sexual satisfaction' and desire for 'more frequent sexual intercourse' among his couples after the operation.

Protestant Christian participation was encouraged by the Archbishop of Canterbury, Dr David Coggan. He urged Indian Christians to accept sterilization because 'it was for the national good'.

Catholic participation received no such holy boost. On the contrary the Vatican periodically expressed concern at what was being done in India under the guise of family planning. An article in a Vatican sponsored magazine attacked the Indian health authorities for harrassing Catholics. Naturally, all these reports were kept out of the newspapers.

The numbers game was yet to reach its dizzy climax. In the third week of September, the Government announced an official family planning fortnight beginning from October 1. The results achieved during these fourteen days are truly staggering. Because they speak their own tale they need only documentation. One surgeon in Chaibasa, Bihar performed 92 tubectomies in one day, thus establishing an all-India record. 9,500 sterilizations were carried out on a single day in Gujarat. A new national record was set up with 2,050 vasectomies in 12 hours in Bhalki, Karnataka. 2,000 beggars were rounded up on October 7 from near the Taj in Agra, and on that very day 1,800 were sterilized.

HOW WERE THE F.P. clinics run? With the cool efficiency of a German prisoners-of-war camp or with sensitivity and respect for human dignity?

Rukhsana Sultana is an engaging, articulate and intelligent woman who doesn't mind being in the news. She has a slightly 'nineteenth century attitude towards the lower classes which is compounded of a genuine desire to help, a readiness to blame poor people for their own conditions, and an inclination to serve the public by ordering them about'.

Rukhsana will confidently tell you 'no excesses were committed,' and add as an after thought, 'not at least in my camps.' Miss Sultana ran half a dozen camps in the Jama Masjid area and the one which acquired the most notoriety was 'Dojona House', financed by those well-known philanthropists and population controllists, 'The Kabari (waste paper) Merchants Association.'

Rukhsana's version presents Dojona House as a festive, relaxed and enthusiastic house. At 10 o'clock tea was served, at mid-day a meal was provided for all. Motivation was done exclusively through friendly talks on loudspeakers. Film music would be interspersed between appeals of 'aao nasbandi karao'. Clocks and Dalda tins were prominently displayed to catch the eye. When a volunteer came forward to be doctored—'I can't stand the word operation,' says Rukhsana—he was first given a cup of tea and something to eat, then he was asked to fill in an application form, and then this application was minutely scrutinized. 'Very often we said, 'no'. At an average we refused thirty people a day,' claims Rukhsana.

Rukhsana keeps handy a bunch of rejected applications which have notings like: 'too young', 'too old', 'politically motivated', 'not necessary'. 'We were not butchers just chopping up people,' she declares angrily.

In the clinic itself, according to Rukhsana, there were six beds and a team of surgeons led appropriately by a Dr Nirodh

Bannerjee. Qualified nurses ensured that strict hygiene was maintained. Approximately 130 operations were performed daily.

The rejected application forms, if genuine, seem to support Rukhsana's contention that she was not indiscriminately chopping up people. However, if you talk to those living near and around Dojona House, you will hear hundreds of hair-raising stories of barbarity and coercion.

Rukhsana has a straightforward explanation for this discrepancy in version: 'There was a huge slander campaign against me and Sanjay. The old Congress leaders like Subhadra Joshi couldn't stomach the idea of someone going into their territory and actually doing something. They were jealous of me. Really the people of the walled city love me.'

During our conversation Rukhsana suggested I accompany her to dinner. She was going to meet the people who worked her camps and I could ask them myself if any excesses had been committed. It sounded like a good idea.

'Where are we going?'

'Jama Masjid,' she replied blandly.

I must confess my enthusiasm for the dinner diminished rapidly. Earlier, I had spent the morning talking to the people of Jama Masjid. Feelings ran high. One aggrieved, bearded citizen, told me to deliver Rukhsana a message: 'Tell her if she ever comes back here we'll lynch her.'

We drove down from Miss Sultana's Connaught Place residence around eight, and although it was dark, Rukhsana's much-photographed, dark-glasses persona was wildly conspicuous. Driving down the meandering lanes of Jama Masjid, by itself a hazardous operation, she was noticed repeatedly with pointed fingers. Each time someone glared at us I clutched my seat; she was as cool as a cucumber.

I was not exactly sure of our destination, but presently the car stopped with three or four ferocious looking gentlemen surrounding it. Rukhsana was given a royal welcome. 'Look how much they love me,' she said as we were ceremoniously whisked away up some stairs to a room where more ferocious looking men and a dining table awaited us. 'These are my workers,' Rukhsana announced proudly, 'ask them, ask them, if any atrocities were committed.'

Dutifully, each man stood up and said his piece. No atrocities. How could there be with a humane person like our Rukhsanajee running the camps? We had dinner. 'Now do you believe me?' asked Rukhsana.

A little later I asked her who these men were. 'They are Rajasthani Nayaks. You see him, he is their leader. Do you know he has committed eight murders and not a single body was found.' She then turned to the leader: 'So how many people did you murder—eight or more?' she asked jocularly. The leader merely blushed. I observed the man. One of his hands was shrivelled up like a cabbage and he had three fingers missing. 'All that happened while he was committing his murders.' Pointing to the others she said, 'These are all his sons and relatives. They too have committed murders and robberies.'

So these were the people running Rukhsana's humane and voluntary sterilization camps!

The truth, and this might come as news to Miss Sultana, is that what began as incentives and disincentives soon degenerated into humiliation and terror. The Lt. Governor of Delhi, Kishen Chand, in April '76 sent a circular to all government offices, schools, colleges, to departmental heads of the Delhi Administration, civic bodies and public sector undertakings. The circular was crisp and clear: All those having more than two children would have to get sterilized or suffer the consequences of no promotion, no confirmation, no increment, no entitlement to government housing, no loan advances, no leave. Meanwhile, those who had two children had to sign the following undertaking: 'I hereby declare that I have at present two children and I hereby undertake to restrict my family to two children. In the event of break of this undertaking I understand that I get exposed to any penalty that may be prescribed by the competent authority.'

School teachers were singled out for special harassment. Each had to motivate a minimum of five people and unless he or she fulfilled the minimum quota salary was withheld. Frequently a hapless teacher would buy a 'bakra' or two for three hundred rupees each to complete the quota.

To ensnare those who weren't government or quasi-government employees there were other incentives. Renewal of driving, rickshaw, scooter, arms, sales tax licence, any kind of licence finally, depended on being able to produce a sterilization certificate. (Around this time gangs of sterilization certificate forgers proliferated all over India. One such gang arrested in Delhi confessed that they had recently switched over from university certificate forgery to sterilization certificates because of demand and better price). Free medical treatment in hospitals was suspended unless one could produce the magic piece of paper. Feroza, a 26-year-old Jama Masjid widow with four children recounts how she lost her 32-year-old husband, Shijauddin. 'My husband had T.B., but they refused to admit him in Pant Hospital till he had himself sterilized. We appealed saying he was too ill to undergo the operation. But they did not listen. So he got himself sterilized, but he was so weak after the operation that he never recovered.'

Another method used to 'motivate' civilians was to arrest those who looked destitute or homeless on the charge of vagrancy. These unsuspecting people would be kept in lock-up for a night and next morning taken to one of the camps for sterilization. This practice became so widespread that it led to an almost total disappearance of casual labour from Delhi. In September '76 for example, if you asked a contractor to whitewash your house, he would refuse on the excuse that his labourers had gone to their villages for Diwali. This was only partly true; the labourers had gone back to their villages, but not for Diwali, they had fled from fear of being arrested for vagrancy.

But there was no respite in the villages either. 'Medical teams used to raid villages, often at night and carry off males to sterilization camps. Those who resisted were sometimes beaten... Fear of the raids rose to such a point that entire villages would flee into the fields at the sound of a jeep coming down the road.'

In Amethi, for instance, men hid at home during the day and in the fields at night. The main market of Gauriganj, in keeping with other town markets, closed down because no one dared come in for fear of being trapped by sterilization teams.

An innocent pastime like going to the cinema became a calculated risk. You never knew when the doors would be locked after the show and the 'patrons' herded into trucks en route to camps.

Before presenting the horror stories portfolio—a relatively easy task now—one should, in the interests of veracity, concede that some reporting excesses were also committed, and thus, concede in part Sanjay's charge that 'the excesses have been grossly exaggerated'.

However, one has to be as simple-minded and as dangerously naive as Sanjay to believe that 'there were no anti-feelings to the programme in itself. It wasn't the nasbandi that caused any resentment. It was just that in certain cases, the after-care was not provided. And the only complaints I received were from people whose stitches had not been removed. The 'statistics' that are being published about forcible sterilizations are fabricated. Not a single case of forced nasbandi has been reported to me.'

It is true that while the programme was being ruthlessly implemented, Mrs Gandhi warned her chief ministers against the use of compulsion. She stated more than once: 'Anyone engaged in harassment while propagating family planning will be punished.' Dr Karan Singh, while acknowledging that several cases of excesses (an 18-year-old youth had been sterilized by 'mistake'; the operation had been reversed) had been reported to him, attributed these to the over-enthusiasm of field staff in their efforts to motivate people. He too spoke of punishments for coercion.

Sanjay listened to these warnings with bemused silence. He told one of his aides that considering the size and radical nature of the programme, the excesses had been minimal. 'Some excesses are inevitable,' he said. Sanjay, however, was opposed to Karan Singh's advocacy of 'gentle and civilized' pressure. Without 'stiff and harsh' penalties he saw no hope for success.

I spent some time in Jama Masjid and Muzaffarnagar, and the figures I collected from these areas varied wildly. One local told me that in Rukhsana's Dojona House camp 500 people had died due to negligence on the operating table, another mentioned a figure of 200, another spoke of thousands. Coincidentally, that very day Mr Raj Narain had made a statement in the House in which he revealed a total of 207 sterilization deaths in the entire country! In Muzaffarnagar (after the riots) I was given a casualty figure of 400. One shopkeeper swore he saw '75 bodies' himself. Interestingly, Mr Charan Singh places the casualty figure at 57, Mr Kuldip Nayar in his *The Judgement* at 25, *Time* and *Newsweek* at 40. Talking to local people, a good rule of thumb I discovered was to divide their figures by ten to arrive at the truth.

This seemingly arbitrary arithmetic on my part is not motivated by a desire to minimize or belittle the havoc wrought by sterilization in the lives of ordinary people. It would, nevertheless, be useful to remember that censorship and its concomitants compel exaggeration. I divide only to counter word of mouth multiplication—an exercise which still leaves enough evidence to confirm the indictment of pressure, intimidation and outright violence.

Here is a sample of the horror stories.

Kartar was a cobbler. One day six policemen walked into his house and told him that B.D.O. sahab (block development officer) wanted to see him. Kartar and his wife went to the B.D.O. who asked Kartar how many children he had. 'I told him that I had four children, three girls and a boy, and I was planning to get sterilized. But that day my son was sick and I said I wanted to take him to the hospital. The B.D.O. got very angry and dragged me into the jeep. When my wife begged him not to take me he threatened to have her sterilized as well. On route to the clinic, the police stopped a man on a bicycle and asked him whether he had been sterilized. When he said no, they hauled him into the jeep leaving his cycle in the middle of the road... After the operation there was an infection and pain. I couldn't work for many months.'

40-year-old Gyani Ram was forced to undergo a vasectomy and then was denied a certificate when it was discovered he was childless.

In Katauli a tea shop owner was ordered to submit to vasectomy or 'we'll burn your shop down'. Helpless, he agreed even though he was 58 years old.

Shahu Laxman Ghalake, a poor peasant, was lifted from Barsi near Sholapur. When he protested that he'd already been operated, he was kicked and beaten. Ghalake even told the doctor that he'd had a vasectomy but he refused to listen. Inevitably he was sterilized again.

In Pipli, a 25-year-old widower, Hawa Singh, was forcibly taken from a bus and sterilized. He died of infection a little later. When the B.D.O. and the police returned for more cases to the village, the women beat them off with broomsticks and rolling pins. An official warned: 'Bombs will be dropped on your village unless you cooperate.' A 70-year-old Harijan was dragged to the clinic: 'I have no teeth, I am going blind, my child producing days are over, yet they made me go through the painful operation.'

In Lucknow a middle-aged man was picked up from Aminabad. All the way to the clinic he kept insisting that he'd had a vasectomy done a couple of years earlier; he even had a certificate at home which he was willing to produce. The police refused to believe him. They brought him to the clinic, and it was only after he had been cut up that the truth of his statement was discovered.

Uttawar is a village 80 kms south of Delhi with a population of Meo Muslims. At 3 a.m. one morning, the inhabitants of the village were awakened by police loudspeakers which ordered all the men to assemble at the bus-stop on the main Nuh-Hodad road. Frightened, unsure, the villagers did as they were ordered, and it was only when they arrived at the bus-stop that they discovered that their village, like in some crazy western movie, had been surrounded.

400 men assembled at the bus-stop, but the police suspected that some were still hiding. In the process of unearthing more volunteers, the police pillaged, broke and looted. 'They behaved like savages,' remembers Abdul Majid. These 'find and operate' activities continued for three weeks in which a total of 800 sterilizations were notched up; and Uttawar 'had the dubious distinction of probably having every eligible male sterilized'.

You couldn't bottle up a nation with this kind of barbaric treatment and not expect an explosion. The first major family planning riot took place in a small town called Muzaffarnagar in U.P., a state whose quota of 400,000 had been raised to 1.5 million by the Sanjay-saluting chief minister, Tewari.

Anger had been seething for some time in Muzaffarnagar. The sterilization clinics, recording 6,000 operations a day, were controlled by the district magistrate (he has been transferred since). He began his campaign by systematically rounding up the Muslim kasais (butchers), and one must record that the predominantly Hindu police did the job with relish. It was a toss up between a sterilization and a communal riot.

On October 16, the police seized rickshaws and roadside stalls in an attempt to force their owners to undergo sterilization. A crowd of 200 gathered demanding return of vehicles; there was a lathi charge.

This, however, was just a foretaste of things to come. On October 18, the police with their customary abandon, picked up 17 'volunteers', nine Hindu, eight Muslim. Such pickings-up were not unusual; what was unusual was the fact that this group included two men over 75 and two boys under 18.

Word quickly spread around the city. A secular crowd of several hundred surrounded the police station demanding return of hostages. The D.M. was adamant. 'Today I will fuck their mother' (an expression which is much more colourful in the original Hindi) was his response. To disperse the crowd the police used tear gas shells, the crowd replied with stones. The inevitable stampede followed, shots were fired in the air and then at the rioters. 30 people were slain and 80 policemen injured.

That very day a citizens' committee was formed in Muzaffarnagar. A call was placed to the Congress president, D. K. Barooah, by which he was apprised of the happenings. Barooah confessed he was helpless, he suggested it would be better to talk to 'High Command'. A call was then placed to 1, Safdarjung for the Prime Minister, and it was routed as usual through R. K. Dhawan. When he heard it was from Muzaffarnagar he promptly hung up.

'It's all lies. I have the file here. No one was killed,' said Sanjay when confronted with the Muzaffarnagar news.

Initially, the government refused to acknowledge any casualties at all. The district magistrate dismissed the incident as a 'minor disturbance' in which a few policemen had been injured. Meanwhile both B.B.C. and Reuters broke the news, reporting the casualty figure at 100. A few days later, Mrs Gandhi was forced to concede in the House that a riot had, in fact, occurred in Muzaffarnagar in which 74 policemen had been injured. Still, no casualties were acknowledged. People wondered how you could have 74 policemen injured in a riot without civilian deaths!

Opposition parties staged a protest outside Parliament. They met President Fakhruddin Ali Ahmed and demanded a judicial enquiry. The president heard them out and sent a copy of their memorandum to the Prime Minister.

The riots spread from Muzaffarnagar to Sultanpur (8 killed) to Meerut to Gorukhpur (1 killed) and by the end of October 'disturbances' had also occurred in Haryana, M.P., Bihar, West Bengal, Punjab and Maharashtra resulting in over 50 deaths.

It was becoming increasingly clear that the Muslims would have to be pacified; they were the one community who were fighting (sometimes literally) nasbandi openly. While states all over India were proudly and loudly announcing their record figures, Sheikh Abdullah's state was conspicuously and understandably silent: Jammu and Kashmir had achieved only 12 per cent of its annual quota.

A campaign to woo the Muslims was launched. The district magistrate of Aligarh offered a new Ambassador car to any person motivating 500 cases (there is no record of anyone claiming the prize). More specifically, the help of religious leaders was sought to alleviate resistance. Statements from revered and learned Muslims declaring Islam's approval of family planning were regularly splashed in the press and the government-controlled radio and television.

It was Rukhsana Sultana, again, who produced the master stroke. She managed to produce two imams (priests), Shareef Ahmed and Noor Mohammed, and persuaded them to undergo vasectomy. The fact that the imams had agreed to an operation was a coup by itself; Rukhsana compounded her success by announcing that these god-fearing gentlemen were natives of Muzaffarnagar.

According to press reports the imams were at first hostile to the idea. Rukhsana, however, quoting passages from the Koran and using her well-known persuasive powers, was able to convince the priests. Indeed, once convinced 'they immediately asked for sterilization, taking priority over scores of people waiting to get sterilized'.

Sanjay was at hand. He signed the motivation cards of the imams, handed them their certificates and the special cash award of Rs. 101 each. Noor Mohammad and Shareef Ahmed on their part assured Sanjay 'that they would do their best to motivate other religious leaders as well'. The following morning, almost every newspaper carried a picture of Sanjay standing between the two sterilized Muslim priests.

Actually, the definitive solution Sanjay proposed for India's mounting population was compulsory sterilization. He wanted the Centre to enact a law which would make sterilization mandatory for couples having two or more children.

Mrs Gandhi, very astutely, decided to distance herself from such a law. She publicly announced that while she was in favour of incentives and disincentives she was opposed to any form of compulsion. However, and this is crucial, she said she would leave it to individual states to make the final decision.

Mrs Gandhi's ploy was obvious. She wanted the states to make the running on the bill. If successfully implemented, she could take credit for it; if not, she could always, say, 'I warned you against compulsion.'

Five states, Punjab, Andhra Pradesh, Maharashtra, Haryana and West Bengal seemed most keen on the idea, and three, Maharashtra, Punjab and Andhra Pradesh, began drafting legislation. Only Maharashtra finally produced a draft, and the state became, in the words of the *New York Times*, 'The first political entity in the world to legislate population control by forced sterilization.'

Maharashtra's keenness to be the standard bearer of Sanjay's new plan was, in a sense, understandable. The chief minister, S. B. Chavan, had on more than one occasion been 'taunted' by Sanjay about his state's poor showing on the sterilization table. Sanjay pointed out what had been achieved in the other states of India. Why was Maharashtra lagging behind?

Chavan, aware of Sanjay's ability to unseat chief ministers, decided to make amends for past lapses. He ordered the secretary to the Public Health Ministry, Palnitkar, to prepare a compulsory sterilization document—and quickly. Palnitkar burned the midnight oil studying statute books, consulting lawyers, doctors, civil servants and politicians. In ten days he had the first draft ready.

The main provisions of what was called 'The Family Size Limitation Bill' required men up to the age of 55, and women up to 45 to be sterilized within 180 days of the birth of their third living child. The first obligation for the operation was placed on men and they would only be exempted if a doctor could certify that a vasectomy would endanger their lives. The bill provided a prison term of two years for those who failed to be sterilized. Dr D. N. Pai, director of family planning, Bombay, clarified that in practice 'offenders would be sterilized and paroled'.

Pai conceded that Mrs Gandhi's half-hearted support for enforced sterilization was a set-back. Nevertheless, he was happy that 'her son is all for it'.

The bill was passed by both Houses of the Maharashtra Legislature, and was awaiting the president's approval when elections were announced. One shudders to think what additional atrocities would have been committed in its name had it been on the statute books.

The story of all the accumulated evils of nasbandi can best be summed up by a single statistic: 270. This was the number of days Sanjay Gandhi's population control programme flourished in India. If sterilization was, above everything else, the central issue on which Mrs Gandhi lost the election, then it must have been an awful and ubiquitous brutality, which in the space of nine months toppled a party with a 30-year unbroken record of rule and a history that went back nearly a century.

Before June '76 the Emergency was a peripheral phenomenon in rural India. The constitutional changes, detention of opposition leaders, curtailment of fundamental freedoms, censorship of the press, were hardly likely to affect the life of the Indian peasant. Why, even Mrs Gandhi's brave, new 20 point programme with its emphasis on freedom for bonded labour and easy rural loans didn't percolate down to the village level.

In February '76 a Bombay monthly, now undeservedly extinct, sent a reporter to the interior of Maharashtra to determine what impact the Emergency had had at the grassroots level. The reporter returned with the not unexpected news that most of the villagers didn't even know there was an emergency in the country.

This ignorance was rudely shattered with the launching of the sterilization programme. And it was this which took the Emergency to the heart of India, to its hamlets and small towns. Without nasbandi Mrs Gandhi (Sanjay?) would still have been prime minister—a conclusion not completely fanciful, but based on the assumption that the imposition of the Emergency would have cost the Congress only the urban vote, the rural vote, as always, would have gone to the cow and the calf.

However, it is the long-term and not the immediate impact of Sanjay's sterilization programme which is the more permanently damaging. After all he did make 14 out of a total of 104 million couples unfertile, an achievement which no doubt will have a steadying effect on the population graph. No, the real danger is that we will revert not to the pre-Emergency lackadaisical approach to family planning but to something much worse, i.e., total inactivity.

Political parties in India have always harboured suspicions about the electoral mileage in interfering with natural procreation. A Congress politician told me that any attempt to curb population growth in India was a 'vote loser'—a conviction which must have been further strengthened by the way Mrs Gandhi was treated by the voters in the last elections.

It is not for nothing that the new Janata government has put Mr Raj Narain where he is. An imaginative and honest government would have realized that if any ministry needed dynamism, subtlety, foresight, authority, it was the Health ministry. What was required was a minister who could stand up and say that sterilization, with incentives and disincentives, was vital to the existence of the country and should be preserved (of course without intimidation). Instead, we have a minister who believes: 'If I pay a man Rs. 100 to have an operation that in a sense is compulsory sterilization, that is a bribe.' Meanwhile, Mr Narain hopes to reduce India's mounting population by reading verses from the Ramayana. A letter to the editor in the *Indian Express* makes the final point: 'If India is to be saved from the catastrophe of a population explosion, Mr Raj Narain should be muzzled.'

What the Janata government has done by making the victor of Raibareilly Health Minister is devalue the ministry itself and relegate family planning to the bottom of its list of national priorities. One does not deny Mr Raj Narain's many-sided competence; he may be excellent with some other portfolio. However, his presence in his current ministry will ensure a reactionary and antediluvian approach to India's most pressing worry.

Politicians and political parties at the best of times touch family planning in India warily. Mr Sanjay Gandhi has made certain, that for a long time to come, no party will touch the problem at all. That is the true measure of the damage Sanjay has done to the country.

The Selling of Sanjay

'Sanjay is a man with broad shoulders. His waist is like that of a lion. What a broad chest! About 36' when empty. When full it takes a very good expansion—say three to four inches... His lips are naturally red. Roses are blooming on his round and smiling face. Sometimes he uses spectacles also. They enhance the beauty of his facial features. Sanjay's smiles are extremely sweet and they go on for miles and miles. They make everyone happy all the while. His eyes look like the shining petals of the lotus. His ears look like pearl shells'.

—Piare Lal Sharma in 'The World's Wisest Wizard'

'HOW,' SAID THE SANJAY crony, 'can you rent a crowd of two lakhs?' He paused for effect, had a sip of his drink and amplified. 'I was with Sanjay in February '76 in Calcutta, we had over one hundred and fifty thousand people.[1] These are not my figures, you can check with *The Statesman*. Now you can rent thirty, forty, fifty thousand people, but you can't rent a lakh and a half.'

The crony was spiritedly answering my charges of crowd hiring. I reminded him of what I had personally seen: two men seated on a raised platform. In front of them are piles of loose one rupee notes and 50 paise coins; behind them is a vast queue. As each person steps forward he is given one note and one coin, and herded into a waiting truck. As each truck gets full it speeds off. The whole operation is supervised by policemen without the slightest suggestion of disorder or confusion or pushing. Besides Rs. 1.50 there is another rate of Rs. 3. The latter is meant for a select group of cheerleaders, the men who will spontaneously throw flowers and spontaneously shout: 'Sanjay Gandhi zindabad,' 'Desh ka neta—Sanjay Gandhi'.

I also tell him a story, not necessarily apocryphal, about the crowd, rented by the hour, which demanded over-time when Sanjay was a couple of hours late for a public meeting.

Only the faintest of smiles crosses his face. 'Of course some of this is true,' he acknowledges. 'Some people may also have come to see a tamasha, but I tell you a lot of people came because they wanted to see and hear a great national leader.'

Great national leader? That certainly wasn't what Sanjay was when he was campaigning for his mother in '71. Then he was lucky if he could get 200 people to listen to him. The same number presumably would have gathered had Mr Sanjay

---

1 Sanjay himself says that 'nobody was ever paid to attend any of my rallies. If the people came in hundreds it was because of curiosity value. They wanted to find out what I was all about.'

Gandhi decided to address a meeting on 24 June 1975. How did he then command audiences of lakhs a year later?

However spurious it may have been, there is little doubt that by mid '76 a Sanjay cult had been successfully planted and promoted. The brief of this chapter is to examine what part the media played in creating and fostering this cult.

The government-controlled radio and television, naturally, were first off the mark. Vidya Charan Shukla made sure of that.

Although, traditionally, individual radio and TV stations have some autonomy in programming, news and commentary are the exclusive domain of the Directorate General. No local station can initiate anything in this area without clearance from Delhi. Thus there was centralised control which made it relatively easy to manipulate content.

In early 1976, TV and radio stations all over India were issued two guidelines. Firstly, they were asked to ensure that 'positive' publicity formed the basis of all programming. The word positive in fact was being bandied around increasingly those days. Mrs Gandhi, Sanjay and senior Congress ministers constantly complained that the Indian media, too, had succumbed to the cardinal western vice: India bashing, or the bad-news-is-good-news syndrome. For a change, said Mrs Gandhi, why not spread the good news.

The only problem was there wasn't any genuine good news to spread around. So it was left to the ingenuity and creativity of individual producers to manufacture it.

The second guideline was more specific. Every programme section was asked to incorporate one or more points of Mrs Gandhi's 20-point and Sanjay's 5-point programmes into its schedule.

For example, you could make Sanjay's passion for beautification the nucleus of a feature. A TV or radio crew would be sent into an area which had been beautified. They would then carefully select and film half a dozen people guaranteed to praise the project. This would be followed by a studio discussion with someone like Jagmohan who would list other beautification projects, explain their 'positive' attributes, and finally pay tribute to the dynamic and inspiring leadership of Sanjay Gandhi.

Within the profession these kind of programmes were called 'stagings'; and soon producers became expert at this perverse art.

A strict check was maintained. Each radio and TV station had to send back monthly reports to Delhi indicating how much 'positive' publicity had been put out from their centres. These reports were sent to the Information and Broadcasting Ministry for 'statistical tabulation'. Points were awarded to each station and a score-board kept. 'Station heads would get nervous and upset when their scores began falling vis-a-vis other stations. The race for points at the management level affected all operational and production staff.'

Jaipal Singh Jhala, a producer on Doordarshan, Delhi describes the working atmosphere of his station: 'The meticulous process of production was altered to suit the demands of a passing political order; staff members were subjected to gruelling pressure; pre-emptory written orders took the place of dialogue between management and staff; innuendo and half-truth took the place of public information... All in all the camera and microphone were used for lies and distortion.'

Not surprisingly, every lead story in public, current and news programmes had to do either with Indira or Sanjay or their immediate supporters. K.K. Dass's White Paper on the abuse of mass media notes: 'Between 1 January 1976 and 18 January 1977 as many as 192 news items were broadcast about Mr Sanjay Gandhi in the main news bulletins from Delhi alone.'

19 November 1976 was not an atypical day for All India Radio. At 8.30 p.m. a thirty minute report from Gauhati ecstatically elaborated on how a new leader had been born pushing out the senile old guard. At 9 p.m., the fifteen minute English news devoted eight and a half minutes to Sanjay's speech and the reception accorded to him. At 9.15 p.m. on 'Spotlight', a fifteen minute current affairs commentary, a special A.I.R. correspondent at Gauhati examined the exciting implications of the impending Sanjay led Youth Congress rule destined for the country.

A Sanjay visit to adjoining areas of Delhi would cause panic and consternation in Doordarshan. 'Two and sometimes three camera crews were pressed into service. Since Doordarshan, Delhi has only three cameras, and so many of its staff went off in pursuit of Mr Gandhi, the work of the TV centre came effectively to a standstill.'

Following Mr Gandhi and recording his activities on tour was only one part of the hectic exercise; the other was delivery. There were orders that even routine visits had to be telecast that very evening under the heading, 'special report'. Further, once the programmes had been broadcast at Delhi they were to be rushed out to other centres. A Bombay producer told me how trying it was during the Emergency to plan even a day's schedule, leave alone a week. As soon as film capsules carrying titles like 'Sanjay storms Kanpur', 'Sanjay and Youth Congress', 'Each one teach one' arrived they had to be immediately inserted into the evening's viewing, cutting and chopping the announced schedule.

I remember one night getting up to switch off my set at the usual end of transmission, 10.30. Instead of the final 'namaste' a sweet young thing announced an extension of transmission time because of a 'very important' film. The film turned out to be 'Sanjay Gandhi in Haryana', an absurd 40 minute Chaplinesque feature showing Sanjay whizzing from one meeting to another exhorting people to 'talk less, work more.'

When Sanjay went out of Delhi, the I & B Ministry issued detailed and advance instructions to the nearest A.I.R. and Doordarshan stations on how the visit was to be covered.

20 February 1976 saw Sanjay in Calcutta. A fortnight earlier communications with the two station directors there began. As always the guideline was 'maximum publicity.'

Pressure was reinforced through local Youth Congress and Congress leaders. Prafulla Kanti Ghosh rang up A.I.R., emphasized the importance of the visit and repeated Delhi's instructions of maximum publicity.

Understandably, the two Calcutta directors were perplexed and confused. On February 12, one of them wrote to the Director General in Delhi asking for more 'definite' instructions. He reminded his superiors that normally someone like Sanjay would get 30 seconds at the airport and one or two minutes for a public rally.

The station directors' dilemma was soon eased. The reply from Delhi stated that the Sanjay visit was to be treated on par with a prime minister's or president's visit.

'There was a spate of telegraphic, telephonic and telex messages, for nothing was to be left to chance. The news coverage and TV reports had to be flown out for screening at other places the same evening. Arrangements had to be synchronized, minute details fixed up, a fleet of cars to be arranged, camera crews requisitioned as the staff at Calcutta was not large enough...one camera crew was brought from Cuttack and another hired locally. Calcutta TV Centre was directed to fly the news capsule by the afternoon flights to Bombay, Madras and Delhi, so that it could be shown the same evening simultaneously with Calcutta.'

It is not surprising then, that on February 21 the entire recording studio of Calcutta Doordarshan was working on Sanjay Gandhi to ensure that the 'maximum publicity' instruction from Delhi was complied with.

It was imperative that the station director be personally present with the crews covering Sanjay. It was his job not only to ensure that Mr Gandhi got 'sustained and immediate' exposure; he also had to be 'seen' doing that job.

Three other government agencies, Directorate of Advertising and Visual Publicity (D.A.V.P.), Press Information Bureau (P.I.B.), and Films Division (F.D.) were also involved in boosting the Emergency. D.A.V.P. inundated the country with hoardings—'discipline makes a nation great'—culled from Mrs Gandhi's speeches. (These were also used as press publicity.) However, D.A.V.P. concentrated more on promoting the Prime Minister rather than her son.

The P.I.B. likewise was less Sanjay-oriented. It bombarded editors with leaflets and pamphlets on the export boom, industrial peace, buffer food stocks, negative inflation—all, of course, a fallout of the Emergency and Mrs Gandhi.

The son was sold by word of mouth. An unctuous P.I.B. official came to see me once with the disclaimer 'friendly visit.' He praised my magazine, I gave him coffee. 'The articles are first class, first class', he said, 'but there is one thing missing: nothing for the common man.' I asked him to make his point more clearly. 'Why don't you carry something on Sanjay? He is doing so much good for the country.' Mindful of the fact that Sanjay's name had not appeared once in my magazine since 25 June 1975, I prevaricated. 'I will send you something', said the official as he left.

He did. Loads of it. What saved me was Mrs Gandhi's inexplicable decision to hold elections.

If D.A.V.P. and P.I.B. were somewhat subtle, F.D. was not. Almost every Indian News Review had Mr Gandhi planting trees or taking cities by 'storm' or opening sterilization clinics. Many 2-reelers based on the 5-point programme were also made.

State governments did not lag behind. In December '76 Sanjay visited Kothagudamu, Andhra Pradesh for 12 hours. He went ostensibly to distribute free agricultural implements, loans and cattle to the 'weaker sections of society.' The result: a full length Eastmancolour, English, Hindi and Telugu documentary called, 'A Day to Remember.'

Government media had no choice but to submit to the Emergency decrees; the free Indian press did. It had, after all, before 25 June 1975 been a fairly objective observer of and commentator on the Gandhi family. Sanjay did occasionally get a bashing, but he was always a controversial figure. More often he was ignored, which is surprising considering the many shady deals he pulled off for Maruti in the early 70s. Sanjay's contention that he has been, from the very inception of his adult life, the *bete noire* of the press seems to be based more on paranoia than on fact.

When the Emergency was imposed, the Indian press had, like any press under pressure, four possible alternatives.

1) It could close its eyes and ears granting blanket approval.
2) It could oppose.
3) It could work within the constraints of censorship and try to exercise a measure of independence.
4) It could shift focus to non-political issues like films, arts, sports.

It would have been combative, and it would have added inestimably to the gaiety of life, if during the Emergency, the majority of the Indian press had decided to work within the second, third and fourth alternatives. Unfortunately, the majority took recourse to the first.

The acrobatic skills displayed were breathtaking. Overnight, vociferous critics became vociferous heralders and in the memorable phrase of L. K. Advani, journalists 'crawled when they were asked merely to bend' thus enabling Mrs Gandhi to 'stage her successful coup against democracy with amazing ease.'

In the early months of the Emergency, when Mrs Gandhi was busy consolidating her own position in the altered circumstances, not much attention was paid to Sanjay. However, as soon as Mrs Gandhi indicated that she herself was pushing her son into public life and was herself interested in promoting his political career, the press promptly picked him up.

Out of the five national English language dailies, (they constitute the main press in India) three—the *Hindustan Times, The Hindu, The Times of India*—took up the cause most actively. If you examine the *Hindustan Times* between, say, December

'75 and January '77 it will take some searching before you can find an issue without extensive coverage of Sanjay. *The Hindu* became the official Sanjay apologist, and I suppose the kiss of death for that paper was when Mohammad Yunus singled it out for special praise. *The Times of India* frequently published as many as eight stories on Sanjay in one edition. Indeed, the *Times* was so delighted with the young man that it refused to publish even letters to the editor which were mildly critical of him or the programmes he espoused.

Interestingly, these three dailies had before June 25 shown commendable independence and fearlessness. For example, they all asked on June 25 for Mrs Gandhi's resignation after Justice Iyer had refused to grant her an absolute stay. Moreover, they had on their staff some of the best, most professional editorial talent in the country. Yet no rumblings of protest were heard, indeed there seemed to be widespread approval of the new dispensation.

A daily paper, by the very fact of its periodicity, has certain built-in limitations when it comes to cult building. Since it must essentially report news, the most it can do is slant emphasis. Thus you could have four column pictures of Sanjay, you could have reports of his visits splashed on the front page, you could print sterilization figures in bold type, you could write editorials (does anyone read editorials except editorial writers?) on the relevance of the Youth Congress. In-depth analysis, interviews, think-pieces, assessments, profiles—the real moulders and manipulators of public opinion—are the legitimate concern of the weekly, fortnightly, monthly press.

In any evaluation of the role played by the media in projecting Sanjay as a great leader, the conduct of three weeklies cannot be ignored. Doubtless, there were others too who put in their penny's worth, but their part was probably minimal. Incontestably, the loudest heralders of the Sanjay mystique in India were the *Illustrated Weekly of India*, *Blitz*, and *Current*, with circulations of three lakhs, two and a half lakhs (all languages) and twenty five thousand[2] respectively. In India two of these three periodicals would certainly be considered mass circulating magazines.

All three were English language weeklies and run by unusually strong editors; in fact, the personality of the editor and the publication was synonymous. *The Weekly* was Khushwant Singh, *Blitz* was R. K. Karanjia, *Current* was Ayub Syed.

Karanjia is perhaps the most distinguished and agile Indian journalist living today. He has known three generations of Nehrus, he was a confidante of Nasser, he is an ally of the Shah of Iran. In his office he sports informal pictures of himself in conversation with Castro, Kennedy, Krushchev. Those who disagree with his politics, and their number is legion, admire and respect his professionalism. He has been called the Rupert Murdoch of India.

Khushwant Singh is nothing short of a phenomenon. He took over a boring, ineffectual, struggling magazine and turned it into a prosperous, lively, controversial forum for dissent and debate. He is today not only an eminent journalist, he is a media celebrity, a station he confesses he relishes.

Ayub Syed bought over *Current* from the late Dosu Karaka in a mysterious deal. He is less well-known than his other two colleagues, making him the junior partner in the trio. Nevertheless, he exercised an influence, totally out of proportion with his circulation, by virtue of his connections

---

2 These figures have altered since.

with the then ruling party. He has himself been a member of the Congress Party Working Committee, a fact which he didn't exactly hide.

It might be useful to remember that before these three editors scooped up Sanjay Gandhi from oblivion, their energies were concentrated on scooping up Mrs Gandhi. Khushwant Singh, circa 1975, was on record: 'I explored all the so-called alternatives and I've not the slightest doubt Mrs Gandhi is head and shoulders above all the possible rivals. I think she's more honest, more able, more sophisticated than Morarji or Charan or Jagjivan Babu or Swaran Singh put together.'

The rush of Sanjay stories in these three weeklies—as elsewhere—began just after 9 December 1975 with Mr Gandhi's formal entry into the political arena. An interesting aside about all the Sanjay eulogies in the *Weekly*, *Current* and *Blitz* is that the by-line is invariably of the editors themselves. This was a departure from the daily press where the editors had encouraged their staff to make the running while they themselves had kept a low profile. By writing under their own names, Khushwant, Ayub and Karanjia[3] made identification of their papers with their hero total.

Characteristically, Khushwant took off first. Precisely a month before the Emergency he wrote a cover story on the much-discussed people's car, 'Maruti'. It is a long, rambling piece attempting to present Maruti as a thriving, feasible and

---

3 Sanjay recently told a friend that his only friends in journalism were Khushwant Singh and Karlekar, editor *Hindustan Times*. Picking up a copy of *Blitz* he said: 'I can understand the *Indian Express* attacking me, but these people...' Sanjay also spoke harshly against Ayub Syed: 'I never wanted him near me. He pushed himself.'

roadworthy concern. That Mr Singh was wrong on all counts is not so important; journalists make mistakes too. What is important and lamentable is the undisguised effort to strengthen and applaud a project which was conceptually a fraud.

Consider this colossal misjudgement: 'Soon little Marutis should be seen on the roads of Haryana and Delhi and a month later they will be running between Kalimpong and Kanyakumari.' You would imagine the assembly lines at Maruti were buzzing with activity, when, as everyone knows, not a car was coming off them.

There is surely a tinge of disappointment as Khushwant notes: 'The best Sanjay hopes to achieve in the coming months is 12 to 20 cars per month. He is an incorrigible optimist and expects full production of 50,000 Marutis per year in four years'.

In conclusion he comes to grips with the *raison-d'etre* of the scandal. 'The main burden of the criticism against Maruti is that in a short time Sanjay has become a very rich man. This is arrant nonsense: Maruti is not the personal property of Sanjay. It belongs corporately to its innumerable shareholders.' Khushwant then explains the vital difference between the Maruti man and the sons of Birlas, Goenkas, Dalmias, Sarabhais all of whom have inherited their fortunes and empires whereas 'he has made Maruti with his own bare hands'.

By the standards of Emergency journalism, Khushwant's piece, despite its obvious propaganda, is restrained and refined. There is yet no talk of Sanjay the great national redeemer.

He, as we now know, was born on 25 June 1975. And with his birth the Maruti connection, which had been the principal reason for Sanjay news earlier, was snapped. No more was heard about the people's car—till after the elections.

Ayub Syed placed Sanjay in the proper historical context: 'The emergence of Sanjay Gandhi as the central figure in the country's youth movement is a major post-Emergency development.' And what about his physical appearance? 'He is a soft-spoken young man with sparkling eyes and a disarming smile. The thick black sideburns mark him out in a crowd.' His mind? 'He talks in short sentences and chooses his words carefully... He is an affable personality deeply aware of the political and economic situation in the country.' How was he going to eradicate social evils? 'Looking into the beaming faces of young girls, he suggested, don't marry boys who demand dowry. The girls applauded profusely.'

Karanjia took over the baton from here. The 14 February 1976 issue of *Blitz* has two photographs of its editor on the front page. One shows him shaking hands with Sanjay, the other shows him gazing at the new leader admiringly. Karanjia discovers: 'In contrast with the Niagara of nonsense that falls from the lips of our politicians, Sanjay Gandhi is a young man of few, very few words. To him words spell works, action, performance ... This invests everything he says or does with a sturdy, rational common sense... Hence the Right-Left-Socialism-Capitalism controversy. Sanjay has no time for the confounding confusions and contradictions of the warring ideologies that have tied up performance like a Gordian knot. Like Alexander he would cut the knot with the sword should the need arise.'

What Karanjia was doing was endorsing Sanjay's popular aversion to ideology. According to the new messiah '... Just using words such as Right and Left has no meaning'—a political philosophy which the editor of the *Blitz* obviously considered not only profound and original but the answer to India's accumulated ills.

The race by now was on in full flight. If Khushwant published an 'exclusive' interview, Karanjia pronounced Sanjay as 'man of the year' and Ayub Syed dedicated an entire issue to the Youth Congress. How far these weeklies could go, and what possible new means of salutation they could devise, became an intriguing area of speculation. Adjectives had been exhausted, superlatives had been heaped, prophesies had been rashly made, yet the sycophancy stakes seemed nowhere near the finishing line. Sanjay, by all accounts, had the wisdom of Socrates, the charisma of Kennedy, the goodness of Gandhi, the patriotism of Nehru and the pragmatism of his mother. He was the perfect amalgam of the impossible blend: the statesman-politician.

Cult-building, though undoubtedly lucrative in many spheres, makes for bad and grey journalism. I quote three short samples, one each from *Weekly*, *Current* and *Blitz*, to corroborate my point. Note how copy is virtually indistinguishible in the three publications which usually have nothing in common except periodicity.

'Gandhi presided over her (India's) rebirth to freedom; Nehru was the architect of her reconstruction; Indira the executor of the plan; maybe Sanjay will be the engineer of the grand enterprise.'

'Sanjay Gandhi has added a new dimension to political leadership; he has no truck with shady characters or sycophants, he is a teetotaller, he lives a simple life, he speaks little—his words are not hot air but charged with action.'

'This man of action turns 30 on 14 December 1976. Within a brief period of 12 months he has reshaped the political texture of the country.'

Each of these editors had one supreme moment. Khushwant Singh on 15 August 1976 published a lead story under the title 'The man who gets things done'. 'He is 29, of medium height and honest eyes ... Despite his receeding hairline he is an incredibly handsome young man... He has roused the conscience of young people against taking dowry, he has injected a sense of urgency into controlling the rate of growth of population control, planting trees and finding jobs for the unemployed; he has shown how coils of red tape can be untangled or shorn, how smugglers, black marketeers and corrupt industrialists, officials and party men can be brought to book.'

Karanjia's finest hour was on 27 November 1976. 'Congress is dead ... Long live the Congress' he wrote in a front page despatch from Gauhati. ' So Sanjay Gandhi's rise to power came to us as history's own answer to our prayers. Here at last was a young man uncontaminated by the political inhibitions and spiritual decadence of the past, capable of mobilizing India's neglected youth power into a million-muscled Land Army ... Nothing short of the dialectics of national evolution can explain this phenomenon... Gauhati has confronted India with its moment of Truth.'

Mr Ayub Syed: 'He has electrified the nation with his fearless call for breaking fresh ground ... He handles situations firmly with an unflinching faith in the country's destiny. He has no room for sycophants[4] ...The impact of his personality has been felt in almost every walk of life.'

Presently, *Current* and *Blitz* are attacking Sanjay with the same zest and exuberance they once hailed him with. Only Khushwant, bravely, some say perversely, remains loyal.

---

4 Note how all three insist that Sanjay had no time for sycophants, when in fact he had a great deal of time for them.

Meanwhile, it is a sad, but instructive sight to observe hordes of journalists who had eagerly jumped on the Sanjay bandwagon disembarking equally eagerly. The truism about adversity being the true barometer of friends has seldom been more chillingly confirmed.

Can I add here my own hesitation and reluctance at singling out three senior and esteemed colleagues for special blame? They probably have sound reasons for their behaviour during the Emergency. Khushwant still thinks that in Sanjay we have a potential leader, he still thinks that that leader was 'used' and 'destroyed' by people around him. Karanjia and Ayub Syed maintain that they were 'misled', that if they had the slightest knowledge of what was really happening under the cover of Emergency they would have broken with both mother and son.

Though commendable, these alibis and justifications don't alter the facts. Moreover, I am not examining motives, I am examining the myriad media forces which catapulted a not too distinguished prime minister's son into a 'great national leader'.

How effective was all the propaganda disseminated by the controlled and free media? There is a school of thought which claims that, since the means employed to sell Sanjay were outstandingly clumsy and unsubtle, they had little or no impact. No doubt it is reasonable to assume that in a society strangulated by rigid censorship and control of news, credibility is the first casualty. The tremendous popularity of the BBC Hindi service during the Emergency underscores that point. Foreign papers too, despite the official charge of anti-Indian, were read avidly since they were among the very few sources of reasonably accurate and factual information.

Persistent distortion turned 'Samachar' into a joke. All India Radio became All Indira Radio, while the reputation of the press dropped to an all-time low. Much of India's urban population was, in varying degrees, aware of the travesty done to the organs of communication. Thus there is some merit in the argument that the massive Sanjay window-dressing was, if anything, counter-productive.

Nevertheless, it is my view that with the passage of time, media credibility would have been restored, in the eyes at least of those who were at the receiving end of that media. One mustn't forget that political propaganda is by definition crude and unattractive;[5] indeed its success is inherent in the simplicity of its themes and its repetitiveness. A small and sophisticated section of the populace may possibly detect the exaggerations and even find them repulsive and grotesque. Many friends told me how alarmed and eerie they felt when Sanjay visited Bombay in mid '76. A calm and purposeful city was transformed into an Orwellian nightmare with the profusion of buntings and arches and hoardings and banners. Yet, the all too visible crudity was essential; indeed one must give credit to the Sanjay sellers for grasping this central fact of cult building.

If you study the creation of 'great national leaders' all over the world you will discover a pattern disarmingly uncomplicated. The halos around Mao-tse-Tung, the Shah of Iran, Kim Il-Sung, Papa Doc, Tito, Kenyatta were not created by subtle and devious Madison Avenue techniques; they were created on

---

5 Orwells '1984' makes the same point brilliantly.

the elementary principle of indoctrination through reiteration. In totalitarian societies a leader becomes omnipotent by being omnipresent. By plastering Sanjay all over the country on all possible media the Sanjay sellers, given another year or so, would have brainwashed a large part of the nation into believing that he was, in fact, a great national leader. What defeated them was not technique but time.

Amethi

OUTSIDE THE RAJA'S PALACE in Amethi stands an ancient and solitary guard. He purports to hold a rifle which has seen happier days, and hanging carelessly around his neck is a bullet belt with no bullets! When the monarch goes for his constitutional evening jeep drive and passes the main gate, the solitary guard gallantly attempts to go through the motions of 'presenting arms' and by the time he finally gets to the prescribed position the jeep and the Raja are 200 yards away. Far from being a deterrent, he is an inducement to plunderers.

The long and splendid durbar hall in the palace is, I notice, in urgent need of dustmen, electricians, darners, laundrymen, carpenters, bulbs, painters. Attired in magnificently regal robes, the Raja's dynastic line hangs solemnly from the fading walls as do the numerous commendations from viceroys and governors for services rendered to buttress the Raj. Despite the ravages of time, the blue, pink and white chandeliers, the Persian carpets, the trophies of shikar, the scrolls of honour, the swords and shields somehow manage to transmit part of the bygone glory and grandeur.

Maharajji, as he is affectionately known, is currently a gentle and wise old man of 76, much dedicated to Hindi literature and tennis. He remembers the Nehrus fondly, even intimately. 'Motilalji was our family lawyer. He fought and won a very important case for my father, a case that went up to the Privy Council in London. Later when it came to my education Motilalji sent one of Jawaharlalji's teachers—an Irishman—for me. We were family friends; it was a great privilege.'

One has only to look up for confirmation of great privilege. Pictures of Motilal, Jawaharlal, Indira (the last two with the present Raja) enjoying Maharajji's hospitality in Amethi abound. A palace hand elaborates: 'Actually it was Maharajji's father who gave Motilal a break in his legal practice by offering him important cases. You could say it was Amethi's money which built Anand Bhavan in Allahabad.'

Once a visitor to Amethi leaves the palace, he is confronted by a species of poverty characteristic of district towns in India. If you arrive by train then the most advanced form of transport awaiting you at the railway station is the *ekka*. I hired one to make a round of the city and I would be guilty of environmental colouration if I said I was shocked or surprised at what I saw. No Naipaulian instances of human deprivation, no buzzards devouring carcasses, no howling dogs, no emaciated children, no grotesque beggars. Conspicuous, however, was a peculiar, almost indefinable quality of backwardness. Not many brick houses, no visible factory, no cycle traffic, no cinema posters, hardly any shops, no banks, not much commercial activity. Even that ever-present symbol of Indian affluence, the transistor, was absent. Little seemed to be happening in Amethi, the town seemed to be engulfed in some pervasive stupor. There was no indication here that India was living in the 70s.

The more concerned and aware citizens of Amethi were aware of its needs and inadequacies: roads, tubewells, industry, schools, hospitals, transport, employment—in fact, a massive infusion of capital was required. The Government, of course, was the only source of capital, but its resources were scarce and even those had to be spread equitably over the nation. Amethi would get its alloted share, in its turn.

There was only one way to jump the queue: make Amethi into a V.I.P. constituency. Prosperity would then pour in the way it had done in nearby Raibareilly. That was one Indira Gandhi miracle which was no illusion.

Actually only one V.I.P. without a seat was visible. And he was much in demand. Constituencies in U.P. vied with each other to secure Sanjay's candidature. Giani Zail Singh continuously 'beseiged' the new leader with requests to stand from Punjab. Mr Vengal Rao repeatedly announced his state's readiness if chosen. Shyam Charan Shukla bombarded Sanjay with telegrams and 'representations' from various parts of M.P., Jagannath Misra entreated with Sanjay to 'grace Bihar'. The whole nation waited 'breathlessly' for Mr Gandhi to pick the seat of his choice.

In April '76, the Raja of Amethi, armed with the five M.L.A.S of the district and the sitting Lok Sabha member, visited Delhi. At a meeting with Sanjay, the Raja personally and officially made the offer. Sentimentality was used as an additional bait.

Maharajji reminded Sanjay that Raibareilly was first his father's constituency and later his mother's. Since Amethi was on the border of Raibareilly wouldn't it be entirely fitting for the son of Indira and Feroze Gandhi to stand from a seat which was so close emotionally and physically to Raibareilly?[1]

'What elections, what seat?' asked Sanjay. 'I don't know when elections will be held. It's too early. I haven't made up my mind yet.'

The Raja's credentials for being the emissary were not exactly impeccable. 'He has played politics all his life, switching from one party to another. Till a few years ago he was a member of the Jana Sangh. Do you know that the present Janata M.P. from Amethi is a protege of the Raja,' a Congress worker in Amethi told me.

Elections or no elections, the Raja and the MLA's kept up the pressure. On 18 May 1976 Vidyadhar Bajpai, the sitting M.P., 'pleaded' with Mr Gandhi to announce his candidacy from Amethi as 'it would create a new sense of dynamism among the people'.

Meanwhile, youth hit Amethi at the end of May '76.

One of Sanjay's more imaginative and successful programmes was 'shramdan'. Young people in groups of one hundred would go into villages and perform 'voluntary labour service'. Things like planting trees, building roads, improving sanitation, digging pits, 'any problem which was not being locally solved' was undertaken.

The traffic of benefits was two-way. The villagers were encouraged and impressed to see 'rich city boys' stripped to

---

1 Actually two of the five Amethi M.L.A. constituencies fall within Raibareilly.

the waist working with their bare hands, and the rich city boys were exposed to the reality of their own country—not text book or rural instructional film reality, but 'real' reality.

In Amethi today even Janata party supporters remember with gratitude the work done by Congress youth camps. At least 28 roads were built, hundreds of trees were planted, a school house was reconstructed. A young boy from Delhi who went to Amethi recollects: 'We were working with the Harijans and I must tell you when we went into their houses we were horrified at what we saw. I couldn't believe that human beings in India were living in those kind of primitive conditions. The women, young and old, had hardly any clothes to cover their bodies. I was worried that some of the boys might get excited at the sight of the nearly naked Harijan women. In fact, nothing like that happened. Instead all of us made a collection and bought sarees which we distributed free to the women. Once I gave Rs. 5 to a sick old man to go to the doctor. He started crying. When I asked him why he was crying he said: 'I have never touched a five rupee note before'.'

Sanjay inaugurated the first of six camps. 'Garibon ka Messiah' (saviour of the poor) said *Samachar* and added: 'He stopped in front of huts to hear villagers' grievances or to acknowledge the blessings of the old with a smile… He infused new hope wherever he went and spread the message of "shramdan"'.

Mr Vidyadhar Bajpai wasn't going to let an opportunity like this go to waste. He gathered the press in Sanjay's presence and once again floated his offer. Would the young leader condescend to select Amethi as his constituency? Sanjay, as usual, was non-committal.

Privately, however, he had by then decided to stand from Amethi. When he would stand he did not know, for it is safe to assume that in the middle of '76 elections were very far from Sanjay's (or Indira's) mind. But he did realize that however distant the elections, he would have to start nursing his proposed constituency—initially by frequent physical appearance.

Thus began a series of Sanjay visits. The *Washington Post* noted in December '76: 'Whenever a small plane lands or takes off— and this does not happen often—from the Fursatganj airport, 15 kms from Raibareilly, people in nearby villages tell each other, "This must be Sanjay Gandhi".' Ostensibly Sanjay came to Amethi or Raibareilly or Sultanpur to plant a tree, or inaugurate a Youth Camp, or launch a literacy drive, or open a hospital, or just tour the area and 'take it by storm'. What he was also doing was ensuring that he was seen and heard in and around the vicinity of the constituency he had selected.

A combination of factors swayed Sanjay in favour of Amethi.

First, and perhaps most important, he knew he would have to stand from U.P. (95 million inhabitants, 85 out of 542 Lok Sabha seats) for reasons of nothing more than political tradition. Uttar Pradesh till then had sired, with the sole exception of the interim Gulzarilal Nanda, all the three prime ministers of India as well as its major politicians. If you controlled U.P. you controlled north India; if you controlled north India you controlled India. That at least had been the pattern of political power prior to '77. Sanjay, equipped as he was with high ministerial hopes, must have grasped this vital geographical fact.

Additionally, Amethi was a safe seat.[2] A Congress stronghold, it had a dominant population of Thakurs and Brahmins, communities which in the past had favoured the Congress. There was, moreover, a sizable Muslim minority, which had also favoured the Congress in the past in the belief that it was the only truly secular party in India.

Sentiment? One cannot assess what part that played in Sanjay's decision. In Amethi, as in Delhi, I was repeatedly told by Sanjay admirers that it was *the* determining factor. I cast no aspersions on Sanjay's reverence for his parents, but a pragmatic, hard-headed individual like him appears unlikely to have great faith in a non-saleable commodity like emotion. If sentiment played any part in the decision its role must have been marginal.

Probably a more swaying reason was the proximity of Raibareilly. Mrs Gandhi's campaign, Sanjay could be sure, would be conducted with enormous skill, panache and money, all three of which he, a novice candidate, needed sorely. There was always the possibility of diverting part of the talent and resources from Raibareilly to Amethi.

The physical proximity of the two constituencies may have been politically useful, but it was more grist to the opposition's mill of jokes and banter. Mr Raj Narain, for example, took great delight in pointing out an ironic parallel: the Congress symbol of the cow and calf, he suggested, was especially apposite considering that mother and son were yoked in adjoining constituencies.

2 Vidyadhar Bajpai had won his seat by over 75,000 votes.

SHUKLA IS A LEAN and garrulous man in his late 30s. Piyush is shorter, quieter and slightly younger. Both are loyal and enthusiastic Congress workers. When Sanjay agreed to contest from their district they were thrilled; the election of the Prime Minister's son meant the salvation of Amethi.

Even before Sanjay arrived, Piyush and Shukla sat late into the night working out the nuts and bolts of the campaign. They knew their town well, they knew the local population well. Given the charisma of a Nehru-Indira connection they anticipated no difficulty in getting their candidate elected. Piyush and Shukla conferred with other Congress functionaries and together a broad consensus was reached on the kind of campaign recommendations to be submitted to Sanjay.

On 5 February, Sanjay Gandhi officially arrived[3] in Amethi and set himself up at the dak bungalow, a quarter of a mile away from the railway station. Piyush, Shukla, the Raja of Amethi, the Raja of Tiloi,[4] Vidyadhar Bajpai and other senior citizens were on hand to receive him.

They had not expected Sanjay to arrive alone. Perhaps he would bring a few advisors, a couple of friends, and of course his wife. Mr Veer Bahadur Singh, a junior minister in the N.D. Tewari government who had been designated as 'overseer', was also expected.

But what Piyush and Shukla did not expect was a horde of aimless, gruff young men doing little except hanging around their master. Piyush carefully welcomed one such man and out of curiosity asked him who he was. 'I am a Youth Congress

3 Sanjay filed his nomination papers on 17 February at Sultanpur.

4 Now the Congress M.L.A. of the constituency.

worker from Haryana,' came the reply. The others too, it soon became apparent, were Youth Congress workers from Haryana, Punjab and Delhi.

The initial reaction of the local Congress workers to the size of the entourage was guarded, though far from hostile. They envisaged the possibility of a happy association between themselves and the outsiders. Perhaps they could work productively as a team.

As soon as Sanjay was comfortably settled in his dak bungalow the local Congress workers went along to pay their respects. Sanjay was polite but perfunctory. He thanked them for coming and hoped that in the weeks ahead he could count on their support. Then he bade them farewell. 'We had gone with so many plans,' said one Congress worker,' we wanted to discuss so many organizational details. We wanted to know what kind of campaign Sanjayji would fight, what would be the thrust of his attack on the opposition. Nothing. He asked us nothing, we told him nothing. We very much wanted to inform him of local feelings, the grievances of the villagers. But he casually dismissed us. Even then we were hopeful. We thought this was a purely social visit—maybe next morning we would get down to serious campaign discussions.'

The next morning there were no serious campaign discussions. Instead, Piyush and Shukla saw a convoy of jeeps with loudspeakers and decorated with posters moving out. The campaign had formally begun with local activists sitting on the sidelines!

If Sanjay possessed a professional team, men with long experience of hustings and intimate knowledge of local terrain, this neglect of the Piyushs and Shuklas of Amethi would have been justifiable. But the Sanjay camp was composed of brash, rude, ignorant and opinionated young fellows whose allegiance even to Sanjay Gandhi was suspect. 'They had,' remembers the Raja of Amethi bitterly, 'no idea of how to fight or organize an election campaign, yet when you spoke to them they talked as if they had been fighting elections all their lives!'

Except for a few close friends even Sanjay did not know those who claimed to be 'helping' him. There were just too many of them; and they were continuously coming and going. 'Once in my presence,' recalls Piyush, 'a man came and told Sanjayji that he had come from Punjab and would like to work in the campaign. Sanjayji accepted him immediately. He did not ask who had sent him or what his name was or what he could do. The man just joined in.' A driver who had been sacked by Sanjay in Amethi for being drunk coolly went off and started working in the Sanjay camp at Gauriganj 12 kms away!

Indeed so much human confusion prevailed that a few Janata workers infiltrated the Congress camp. No doubt they performed valuable intelligence service for Ravindra Pratap Singh. Shukla confesses he even recognized some of the opposition men, but since 'no one was asking my opinion about anything I kept quiet.'

Over the next few days, Sanjay and his friends took complete control over the running and management of the campaign. The only domestic allowed in was the fledgling son of the Raja of Amethi, but for very personal reasons. Simultaneously an impenetrable, protective ring was thrown around the candidate. 'It was impossible to meet him,' recounts the Raja of Tiloi, 'they would ask you questions like: "What do you want?" "Why do you want to see him?" "We will pass on your message", "He is very busy", "Come tomorrow". I felt so humiliated.'

The cabal which isolated Sanjay from his immediate environment included Jodh Singh, Sanjay's sardar bodyguard, Kalra from Maruti, Veer Bahadur Singh, the U.P. minister, Kamal Nath, plus a few other Doon School buddies, Arjun Das and Afsar Hussain, the District Magistrate of Sultanpur. (Except for Afsar Hussain, Arjun Das and Veer Bahadur Singh, none of the others had any previous election experience.) Even the old Raja of Amethi, the moving spirit behind Sanjay's candidacy, found it difficult to break the barrier. 'After some time I just gave up,' he reminisces. Remembers Shukla: 'Not only would they not let you see Sanjayji but they were extremely rude when you made such a request.'

It would be unfair to suggest that Sanjay and his team had no campaign plan; rather they had a campaign plan of such startling simplicity and clarity that one would have thought it was the work of veteran electioneering experts who had made intensive studies of polling patterns in Amethi.

The entire campaign was seen as meeting-intensive; indeed the barometer of success was the number of daily meetings addressed by the candidate.

Each evening, Sanjay would sit with his team and tot up the score. If five meetings had been held on a particular day, the figure fixed for the next day would be seven. 'All one heard from the dak bungalow was "meeting, meeting, meeting!" No one ever spoke about anything else,' says Piyush. By early March, with three weeks to go to polling, Sanjay was addressing anything up to ten meetings a day, and the energies of his staff were even then directed towards devising new ways and means for increasing this number.

There is no doubt in my mind that Sanjay was personally responsible for the direction and format of his campaign. If anyone fancied himself as a veteran election campaigner it was the candidate himself, who in 1971 had spent long nights putting up posters in Delhi for the Congress. Moreover, the people hovering around Sanjay in Amethi had neither the intelligence nor the experience nor the guts to do any original thinking.

As campaign strategy, there was nothing intrinsically wrong with reliance on meetings, provided of course they formed part of a campaign mix, and provided the constituency and the candidate were suitable for this style of electioneering. Alas, Sanjay and his faithful never fully understood either the implications nor the demands of a meeting-intensive campaign.

In rural towns election meetings are conducted at a leisurely, almost festive pace. The audience likes to sit and gossip, it likes to hear a bit of song and laughter, it likes to see local worthies on the dais, and finally it likes a long, detailed, rhetorical dissertation from the candidate. Even if you hurried a meeting in a place like Amethi it would take at least two hours.

With a hectic schedule of ten meetings a day, Sanjay couldn't spare two hours. A police constable from Gauriganj told me that Sanjay would frequently arrive 'before time' and then get greatly upset when he saw no crowd. 'He didn't realize,' said the constable, 'that in places like Gauriganj when you announce a meeting for 9.30 people will start gathering around ten.'

Finally, when the crowd settled down and proceedings began, they were finished almost before they had started. Sanjay made his customary short, lacklustre speech, folded his hands and departed. The crowd was left bewildered. 'I have been to a meeting which began at noon and finished at 12.15,' a local told me.

Sanjay's powers at the microphone stood him at a further disadvantage. If he had been an orator like Raj Narain or Atal Behari Vajpayee he could possibly have electrified a crowd in five minutes. But, as is well-known, he was a pedestrian, uninspired speaker, gifted with no turn of phrase or sense of humour. 'He made the same old dreary speech wherever he went,' says Shukla, 'so if you had heard him once there was no need for you to bother again.'

Not only was Sanjay's campaign meeting-intensive, it was also jeep-intensive. Certainly on the main roads of the constituency there were signs of the candidate's presence, but a major part of the constituency was located off the roads, in areas inaccessible to jeeps. The only way to reach these areas was on foot or bicycle. The smart young men working with Sanjay refused to get their feet wet or dirty. Thus Sanjay Gandhi in a rural constituency fought a largely urban campaign.

The Janata candidate, Ravindra Pratap Singh, was, in every way imaginable, the antithesis of the Congress candidate. Mr Singh has, it is true, a moderately menacing look. The thick curled moustache, full face, bulging muscles, unforgiving eyes, give him the appearance of a 'village tough'. And tough he is.

Legend has it that he eats enormous paans, his favourite sport is wrestling, his passion is malish, his staple diet is meat and roti. If you meet someone from the Congress camp, they are likely to tell you lurid tales of Ravindra Pratap Singh moving around town with his henchmen (frequently drunk) terrorizing and beating up people, and generally acting the role he looks. His father, they say, is no less. Many unproven murders—his own brother!— are attributed to him. Violence, it would appear, runs in the family.

Janata Party hands, understandably, have a different tale to tell. A simple, modest, non-violent, god-fearing, happily married Jana Sangh lawyer eking out a meagre living practicing law in Amethi. His entry into politics was, it seems, fortuitous. 'It all began,' he says, 'with the question of a bad road that linked my village with Amethi. I went to meet the local MLA at the kacheri and asked him to do something about it. He refused, began to haggle. "You want to contest an election with me, that's why you want the road repaired" he said. I tried to explain. He insisted. So I grasped his hand and shook it. The die was cast. I fought the election in 1967 and became MLA.'

A month after the Emergency was imposed, Mr Singh was put in jail. He stayed inside for eighteen months.[5] When the elections were announced he was the Janata Party's natural choice.

Ravindra Pratap's was a cycle-intensive campaign. Students, some of them R.S.S. members from Allahabad and Benares University, came in great numbers. Each morning, in small groups, they would set out to sell their candidate. A village would be selected by two, three, four students. They would arrive and not only campaign intensively but live there—live till such time they were sure that the village votes were in the bag. The impact of eating and sleeping in the village, holding panchayat discussions, answering questions person-to-person gave an intimate, personal air to the campaign.

Alternately, they would select a teashop. Here again two or three activists would unobtrusively insert themselves and initiate political issues while slowly unfolding their party

5 Mr Singh was released on 6 February 1977.

propaganda. 'They would come every day and pretend to drink tea, but whenever anyone came they would start talking politics and praising their own candidate', a teashop owner near Amethi station told me.

How many public meetings did Ravindra Pratap Singh hold? No precise record is available, but by all accounts not more than twenty. 'We did not believe in meetings. Meetings are too impersonal—and frankly we did not have the money Mr Sanjay Gandhi had. Also our candidate was well-known to the people so we did not feel the need to introduce him to the public. Most of our meetings took place when some big personality like Charan Singh or Jagjivan Ram came,' says a Janata worker.

The Congress party all over India was fighting the election on what it thought were serious and substantial issues. The Emergency, courtesy Mrs Gandhi, had showered innumerable benefits on the people of India. Industrial production was up, industrial strife was down; university and college campuses were peaceful; a record buffer food stock had been collected; foreign exchange reserves were at an all-time high; inflation had not only been contained, it had been reversed; relations with foreign countries had improved; and, of course, the trains were running on time. 'The nation was on the move' and the only way to ensure it continued to do so was to vote Congress.

For himself, Sanjay wasn't too certain what the election was all about. In a press conference on 25 January 1977 he seemed in characteristic verbal form:

Q.: Mr Gandhi, earlier you were against having elections. Are you personally in favour of them now?

A.: All in all, seeing things as they are now, it's okay. If you'd asked me six months ago I would have said no.
Q.: What has improved?
A.: Nothing. Six months ago I would have thought to wait longer would have been better—which now I do not think.
Q.: Would you expect the fact of the Emergency to be the principal issue in the campaign?
A.: What do you mean by that?
Q.: Well, recently the Janata party has been talking about the Emergency itself as a campaign issue.
A.: I don't think that would be much of a poll issue. Because most of it has happened. It would be a poll issue if it was going to happen.
Q.: What about family planning? Do you think that will be a major issue?
A.: I don't think so.
Q.: What would you expect would be the major issue?
A,: I am not quite sure.

BY THE TIME SANJAY arrived in Amethi, he seemed to have shed his earlier fuzziness. He had by then perceived the issues. In speeches he would stress the 'package' of progress made during the previous nineteen months, the transformation awaiting Amethi on his election (275 km of hard roads, 1200 km of kutcha roads, a multi-crore textile mill), the disparate nature of the opposition (which usually included an attack on Charan Singh). And then he would come to the programme closest to his heart: family planning via nasbandi. 'As soon as Sanjay mentioned the words "parivar niyojan" and "nasbandi" the audience would get incensed. We could see the anger seething in their faces. Many of those listening had suffered personally and many more had heard the experiences of friends and neighbours. Congress workers would hang their heads down when Sanjay spoke about those things. They did not dare look the people in the face. By his speeches, Sanjay, instead of making people happy, was making them more and more angry,' a Block Development Officer from Jagdishpur told me.

What aggravated domestic sentiments even further was the sight of Afsar Hussain, the District Magistrate of Sultanpur. He was prominently visible in the company of Sanjay, helping to organize meetings, collecting crowds, arranging security, and sometimes even on the dais. Mr Hussain's reputation had spread far and wide as the man who had ordered the firing in Sultanpur on crowds protesting against forced sterilization. Many, the rumours went, had been slain. 'Why did Sanjayji insist on being seen in public with that man—the man we used to call "the butcher of Sultanpur"?' wonders Shukla.

In early March the local Congress workers got together. Something had to be done, someone had to speak to Sanjay. The Raja of Tiloi was deputed as spokesman and he, when he finally managed to secure an audience, made an eminently reasonable suggestion. Why not, purely as election tactics, drop references to family planning and nasbandi in speeches? 'I didn't ask him to abandon the programme or curtail it. I made no criticism. All I said was: "Sanjayji, please don't talk about it in public. People don't like it. You are losing votes each time you speak about it."'

Sanjay would not listen. 'The programme,' he said, 'is a good programme, a vital programme. So what if a few excesses are committed? If it is a good programme why should I not mention it?' Sanjay's faithful, including Veer Bahadur Singh, heartily concurred.

The Centre, meanwhile, dipped into its bag of tested election tricks. Just after polling was announced, the U.P. Government increased house allowances for civil servants and reduced the land levy by 50 per cent,[6] All in vain, however, since the Sanjay election was not about land levy or even the development of Amethi, it was, as the whole nation knew (with the possible exception of Mrs Gandhi and Sanjay) knew about nasbandi. And Mr Gandhi was going around espousing and defending it!

Mismanagement was reflected in other areas. Mr Dilip Kumar volunteered his services for the campaign. His appearance was announced all over the constituency for March 7. Large crowds collected from early morning to 'see' the film star— but he didn't appear. Someone had bungled the dates.

He was, it transpired, supposed to arrive the next day, on which day he did arrive, only to find there was no one to receive him at the Fursatganj airstrip. Transport in Amethi being virtually non-existent, Dilip had to wait for two hours under a *pipal* tree for a bus, which, when it did arrive, dropped him at a teashop. Mr Kumar had a restoring cup of tea and somehow managed to send word. Eventually a jeep arrived to pick him up and a meeting was hastily arranged for that afternoon. Alas, word didn't get around, and the meeting flopped.

Or take the antics of Dara Singh and his band of wrestlers. They were brought in not to campaign but to break up meetings of the opposition.

---

6 Just before the election, land levy in U.P. had been nearly doubled.

On March 11 Jagjivan Ram was billed to hold a meeting in Gauriganj. Arjun Das and Kalra thought it would be a good idea to organize a wrestling match a few hundred yards away 'in violation of the agreed schedule of the day's campaign in that town.' That a fight should have broken out between rival supporters was inevitable. Mr Dara Singh and his musclemen were prominent in the fray and currently there is a case against Dara Singh (for violence and disturbing the peace) pending in the Gauriganj courts. Sanjay, it is said, was furious when he heard of the incident. 'Get them out of here,' he said, but by then it was too late.

A couple of weeks into polling and Sanjay could see that the 'hava' (wind) had changed. He could see it in the faces of the sullen, sparse crowds sitting with Chinese inscrutability at his rallies. Their eyes registered no emotion, their expression suggested no enthusiasm. At the end of meetings, when Sanjay made his customary clarion call: 'Desh hi neta...', only the paid cheerleaders shouted, 'Indira Gandhi'. Reports from other parts of the country brought forth similar gloomy news. (Congress canvassers were receiving neatly reversed replies: 'Bring us two Congress candidates for sterilization and you will get our vote.') Despite massive infusions of money, resources and government machinery, the Congress campaign was just not taking off. 'It will not be easy,' confided Sanjay to a friend.

With knowledge of campaign stagnation, Sanjay made a major concession. Along with public meetings he agreed to undertake a few padyatras—something for which the locals had been agitating. 'If we had had our way, the priorities would have been different from the start; we would have cut down meetings to a bare minimum and put all the stress on padyatras.

In fact this was going to be our suggestion to Sanjayji when he arrived in Amethi for the campaign,' says Shukla.

Sanjay made the concession only in principle. He agreed to padyatras, but insisted on doing them his way—which was to walk through villages at sprint speed while an aide shouted 'Sanjay Gandhi zindabad' on the megaphone. Not only did this create physical problems for those accompanying him, but just breezing through defeated the purpose of the exercise. 'We had expected that Sanjay would go to a village, talk to the elders, have a glass of milk, knock at the few houses. We wanted the candidate to be seen and heard in an informal, personal atmosphere. And we also wanted to exploit the Nehru-Indira name. "Look who has come to talk to you—the grandson of Jawaharlal and son of Indira Gandhi" we wanted to say. But he didn't give us a chance. Sometimes we literally had to run to keep up with him,' remembers a Youth Congress leader of Amethi.

On the few occasions Sanjay reduced his pace and tarried, the response was phenomenal.

When he knocked on the door of an old Brahmin, the man was so overcome that he fell at Sanjay's feet sobbing copiously. 'Please vote for Congress,' requested Sanjay. Unable to speak, the Brahmin nodded his head repeatedly.

A pradhan cut short Sanjay's appeal with his own. 'My son, what are you doing in this heat. Look at your feet. You just go back. Not only will I vote for you but I promise you the votes of the entire village. But you get out of this hot, burning sun.'

Maneka's reception was less effusive. On a padyatra by herself, she was surrounded by angry women and accused of making them bewas (widows). 'Our men are no longer men', the women shouted. The scene threatened to get ugly. An

Indian Express correspondent reported in his paper the hostile reception Maneka got. When this report was shown to Sanjay he said: 'It was nothing to do with me. I was not there. They are not against me but against Maneka.' The person on the receiving end of this extraordinary reply told me: 'I couldn't believe that an intelligent, sane man could have made that kind of remark. Perhaps it is a reflection of his mental calibre.'

Sanjay did not anticipate staying cooped up in Amethi during the entire campaign. He anticipated that he would be whizzing around the country addressing Congress rallies, gathering votes with his formidable presence. Unfortunately, very early on in the campaign, Mr Gandhi's presence at election rallies was found to be counterproductive. The opposition was gunning for him, the press was busy exposing his doings during the Emergency, the crowds did not take to him.

Although the Janata Party knew that, in a sense, the election was about Sanjay Gandhi and his activities, senior leaders like J.P. and Morarjee refused to recognize his existence. 'Who is he? I don't want to talk about him. He is too insignificant,' was Mr Desai's response when reporters pressed him on the subject. Playing the role of the philosopher-statesman, J.P. too discovered he had no time to speak about 'that boy'. Aligned with tactics was contempt.

The second string of Janata leaders did not spare him. (Remember Jagjivan Ram's joke: 'The whole country has been ruled by 1½ bosses.') Nasbandi horrors, Turkman Gate, toppling elected governments, shady business deals, illegal appointments... were all placed at his door. Not surprisingly, the Congress High Command instructed the 'messiah' to confine himself in and around his own constituency. The Congress had enough trouble without him.

Sanjay did, however, manage to slip out. With N. D. Tewari he campaigned extensively in U.P., and he also spent some time in M.P. On March 10 he was at Vidhisha (near Jhansi) where he received his most monumental snub. To a crowd 8,000 strong Sanjay declared: 'In Jhansi once a patriotic queen was killed by traitors. I know there are no traitors among you. Or are there any traitors among you? Put up your hands if you are traitors.' Almost the entire crowd of 8,000 obliged.

If a Congress Gallup or Harris had been present at Amethi from the inception of the campaign he would have detected three distinct time moods in the constituency.

To begin with there was a quantum of pro-Congress sentiment. The bait of a V.I.P. constituency seemed to have worked; roads, tubewells, industry, promised a new era to an area which was among the most backward in the country. In February, Congress canvassers found some receptive audiences—audiences which were attentive and curious; in short, they were buying the Sanjay line.

By early March a subtle shift had taken place. If you quizzed a villager about his voting intentions, and he knew you were from the ruling party, he would in turn quiz you. 'Babujee, you tell me which party I should vote for?' After you had told him, he would say: 'You are absolutely right. I will vote for Congress.' Really, all the man was doing was evading the question politely.

March 10 onwards the final mood manifested itself: total silence. Earlier at least people had made perfunctory enquiries, they accepted and sometimes read the printed hand-outs, occasionally asked for amplification on some question. Now there was a complete hush. When Congress workers accosted voters and reeled off the party line, voters stood motionless and gazed blankly. After the canvasser had finished they would walk off quietly. 'Suddenly,' remembers the Raja of Tiloi 'there was complete sanata. We were making loud noises on our amplifiers but the voters were mum. The silence was stunning. I could feel it as it enveloped the entire constituency. There was no fear on people's faces—they just wanted to be left alone till they had cast their vote.'

A journalist did manage to get through to one local of Jais.

'How has it been for you during the Emergency?'

'We have been living like animals these past months, hiding from nasbandi.'

'Which party will you vote for then?'

'That I cannot tell you. My vote is secret.'

On 14 March after a hard day in the field, Sanjay got down, at his dak bungalow in Amethi, to scrutinize the list of recommended 'polling officers'; the men and women who would ensure Congress interests in the forty or so polling booths spread over the constituency. Two hundred volunteers required selection from a list of five hundred—and Sanjay had to sign the papers of each.

A long, laborious process of vetting ensued. Around 9.30 p.m. he finally finished. A genial soul suggested that since it was nearly bedtime Mr Gandhi might care to sleep in the Amethi dak bungalow. 'But Maneka is alone in Gauriganj,' said the concerned husband.

Four people got into the jeep. Gulzari Lal Kalra took the wheel and next to him sat Sanjay; the rear was made up by Jodh and Veer Bahadur Singh. Usually a security van followed Sanjay, but on this occasion the District Magistrate, Afsar Hussain, struck up a 'friendly chat' with the security staff just as the jeep was leaving. The friendly chat over, the D.M. thought it would be best if the security van did not go at all. 'Mr Gandhi does not like these things.'

10.10 the Jeep was negotiating a sharp crossing near Munshiganj—a turn which would have put it on the Gauriganj road. Sanjay, sitting in front, leaned back to exchange a word with Veer Bahadur Singh when a volley of five bullets 'showered' on the jeep. One of the bullets would in fact have hit Sanjay had he not leaned back. The other four grazed the body of the jeep.

The bullet 'shower' allegedly came from a grey coloured jeep inside which, according to Sanjay, were two men whose faces 'were heavily hidden by towels or cloth wrappers.' Jodh Singh, fulfilling his bodyguard duties, returned fire—three shots—but the 'miscreants managed to escape under the cover of darkness.' They were last seen heading towards Sultanpur.

At 10.45 p.m. the attacked jeep arrived at Gauriganj police station where Kalra filed the F.I.R. A case under I.P.C. Section 307 (attempt to murder) was registered.

The next morning *Samachar* reported the 'providential escape'. The 6 a.m. news bulletin carried details of the shooting with condemnations from the Chief Ministers of U.P., Assam and Rajasthan. In the 8 o'clock news, twelve Chief Ministers registered their horror at the 'dastardly act'. Mrs Gandhi, in Patna, surprisingly, issued a mild protest: 'I am always against violence and I condemn this incident.' From Surat Morarjee Desai too condemned the attempted violence with two reservations: 'How can Congressmen accuse the opposition of having any part in the incident when the police has still to arrest the culprits? Couldn't it be the work of the countless enemies Mr Gandhi has?' The General Secretary of the Janata

Party, Surendra Mohan, dismissed the episode as 'lifted from the pages of fiction by Irving Wallace.'

The shooting story narrated so far is the story according to Sanjay. His supporters maintain that even before the 'dastardly act' Amethi was rife with rumours about possible attempts on Sanjay's life. Akbar Ahmed, a Doon School contemporary of Sanjay who worked diligently and wisely in the election, put to me what he thought was the gut issue. 'If he had to fake a shoot out, why would he have left it so late?' Also, 'If he had to fake it, would he have done it so clumsily?'

Before taking up Akbar Ahmed's contention, it should be stated that the U.P. C.I.D. has still not completed its investigation, and no report—contrary to press reports—has been submitted to the state government.[7] In Lucknow I tried in vain to make enquiries about the progress in investigations. All I got from a C.I.D. official was an ironical grin and, 'Does it sound genuine to you?'

Since the shooting occured, the incident has become turmoiled in contradictions and Hitchcockian mystery. Why was there no security van that night? How did the assailants know there would be no security van? How were the assailants so well positioned? Why have the assailants not been apprehended? Was the possession of a .32 revolver[8] (bought four days prior to the incident) by one of Sanjay's jeep drivers a coincidence? Why did the D.M. state that the

---

7 A U.P. minister has made a statement that the incident appeared to be a fake. On what basis he was making this statement is unclear.

8 The assailants seemed to have used such a revolver for the shooting.

shots were fired from a 'grey' jeep while Kalra in the F.I.R. recorded 'green'? Why the confusion about whether Jodh Singh or Kalra was driving? If the jeep was fired at while in motion, how come the bullet marks on its body are so close to each other? How did A.I.R. get reactions from Chief Ministers spread as far as Rajasthan and Assam for its 6 a.m.[9] bulletin the next morning?

The Sanjay angle on the incident is easily answered. 14 March was not too late to 'fake' the shoot out, indeed it was the ideal date, considering that polling was only two days away: this precluded the possibility of serious denials and investigations. What Sanjay hoped to reap from the incident was sympathy— and if anybody needed sympathetic votes on 14 March, it was the Congress candidate.

The quality of the incident, or clumsiness as Mr Ahmed puts it? Well, a lot of people I've spoken to think the quality of the incident and Sanjay's own imaginative powers coalesce quite nicely. In Amethi, I found Congress workers embarrassed to answer questions about the shooting. The Raja of Tiloi looked up at the ceiling, shrugged his shoulders and said: 'Well, if Mr Gandhi says it happened—it must have happened.' I got the impression that most people thought the shooting at Munshiganj crossing a poor joke.

---

9 Deposing before the Shah Commission, Mr P. S. Kasbekar, news editor of Samachar, stated that his 'only source of information on the shooting was Om Mehta', while S. C. Bhatt, Director, News Services, A.I.R., said that he had received a call from Shukla between 1 and 2 a.m. on 15 March.

In Delhi I traced Jodh Singh, the key man in this drama. He is currently under surveillance and he also claims he has been mercilessly worked over by the police. He refused to talk to me.

March 15 found Sanjay in a distraught and disgusted state of mind. What he reckoned would be a bang had turned out to be a whimper. Except for *Samachar*, A.I.R. and Doordarshan, few took the assassination attempt seriously. Instead, there seemed to be some levity in people's reactions to the shooting.

The difficulty, of course, was that to many Sanjay's 'stunt' had come as no surprise. They saw it as a concluding gamble, a desperate act of a desperate man. A Janata spokesman voiced more than party views when he said: 'We were expecting something like this. When a man is drowning he will do anything to save himself.' Paradoxically, the more the captive media emphasized the shooting, the less credibility it acquired. Sanjay found that instead of sympathy he was on the receiving end of ridicule. And he was angry.

Mrs Gandhi got word—probably through Om Mehta—of her son's state of mind. She despatched the 'flying swami' (Dhirendra Bramhachari) to pacify her son. The swami flew in his private aeroplane on the 15th evening, and, using his mystical-spiritual powers, did manage to calm Sanjay.

Many are convinced that the Amethi shooting was a prelude to massive national disruption. An American paper, *Washington Star*, claims it has evidence that Sanjay was planning large-scale arson in Delhi in order to scuttle the elections. Never completely happy with his mother's decision to go to the country, he had realized by early March that Congress would get annhilated at the polls. Bansi Lal, as usual, is supposed to have been Sanjay's lieutenant in this nefarious plan.

I must confess I found little evidence to support this theory, which, I concede, sounds exceedingly attractive on paper. My own view is that Sanjay's motives for faking the shoot out were limited and rather simple: he hoped to swing some opinion in Amethi to his side. When the locals heard that the big, bad thugs of the Janata had tried to do away with the young, innocent son of Indira, wouldn't they shed a tear? That precisely the opposite happened is further testimony to Sanjay's nearly congenital inability to reconcile objectives and results.

On polling day further bad news awaited Sanjay. From all over the constituency came reports of a massive turn-out. Long queues began forming before the booths opened, and as the day progressed the queues lengthened. (Pundits had predicted that a heavy poll would favour the opposition).

An editor of a national weekly in Amethi found Sanjay on March 16 'sitting in Gauriganj at the Inspection Bungalow directing his team of workers with a large map of the constituency in front of him. The candidate sat behind a large table in a room with one or two officials and with a swami sitting on an easy chair. There was a telephone behind him over which Mr Gandhi gave directions. All around the building were armed guards...'

Once voting was over there was little for Sanjay to do in Amethi. He and Maneka hitched a ride back to Delhi on the Swami's plane. On the evening of March 19, Sanjay returned in time for the denouement—which, on the 21st morning, presented itself as a defeat by 77,885 votes.

THOSE WHO SAVOUR THE infidelity of electorates will, no doubt, relish the irony in the Amethi Vidhan Sabha results declared a few months later: four out of the five MLA seats in the constituency fell to the Congress. Further irony: Tiloi, from where Sanjay secured the least number of votes, returned a Congress nominee with a thumping majority.

Sanjay's defeat, in the final analysis, cannot be attributed to lack of effort or to mismanagement. Personally, Sanjay worked like a man possessed, as did Maneka. A 16-hour day for him was the rule rather than the exception. Despite badly blistered feet he did not, till the very end, relent either the pace or the frequency of his programme. 'If only those hanging around him had worked half as hard, the result would have been different,' speculates Piyush.

Would it have? Almost every Congress sympathizer in Amethi talks extravagantly of poll rigging. Sanjay himself, in private, swears that the sole reason for his defeat was manipulation and fraud at the booths.

Estimates fluctuate considerably, but the general consensus in the constituency is that rigging did take place. (Janata people reluctantly agree, but insist their party had nothing to do with it— it was voluntary rigging.) And why not? If you alienate the complete spectrum of the citizenry, from the peasant in the field to the Raja in his palace, what can you expect? That some of these people would come to occupy key positions in the election machinery was inevitable, and it was also inevitable that they would be fiercely partisan. Moreover, Congress canvassers were chosen from precisely those people—teachers, policemen, village headmen, municipal clerks—who had been pressurized and harrassed to sell sterilization during the Emergency. Thus the situation was ripe for mammoth rigging.

Surprisingly, mammoth rigging did not take place; instead it was restrained, even methodical. If a polling officer, forty minutes before closing, found he had six hundred unused votes, he would stamp three hundred with the Janata symbol and push them into the box. Alternatively, the polling officer would call a Janata worker and mention casually: 'I have three hundred votes left. Do you think you could use hundred?' After they had been appropriately used, the official would say: 'I didn't see anything.' Weren't Congress supervisors keeping check? 'What check? The Congress workers sometimes helped in the rigging,' says the B.D.O. of Jagdishpur.

Evidence for this kind of rigging is all too easily available in Amethi. However, I doubt whether it was crucial in deciding who would finally sit in the Lok Sabha. Perhaps the margin of defeat would have been different, but not the result. My own estimate is that Sanjay would have lost by 60,000 instead of 77,000 votes.

It is a fact that on polling day Ravindra Pratap Singh loudly and publicly proclaimed: 'It doesn't matter if I lose here, I will win the (election) petition.' The Sanjay camp cites this as an admission of despair and defeat on the part of the Janata candidate—a defeat which became victory courtesy huge rigging.

The interpretation is too facile. Mr Singh, one can be sure, was more concerned in pointing out the massive and blatant use of government personnel and machinery in the Congress campaign. If Mrs Gandhi could be disqualified for a few rostrums and one government servant, her son, who had everyone from the B.D.O. to the District Magistrate working for him, would surely be unseated by the courts.

In the course of writing this book, I have talked to many intelligent people about why Sanjay lost. From among them I shall not easily forget a conversation I had with a Ravindra Pratap aide in Delhi. After briefing me extensively on his party's campaign in Amethi he whispered conspiratorially into my ear: 'I'll tell you something Mehta sahab. Such was the hava in Amethi during the elections that even if we had put up a donkey against Mr Sanjay Gandhi, we would have won.'

Getting to Know Her 'Achilles Heel'

BEFORE ANYTHING ELSE, I better make absolutely clear that I did not meet Sanjay Gandhi during the course of writing this book. In fact I have never met Sanjay Gandhi in my life. I have seen him in photographs, in newsreels, on television screens, but I have never met him in flesh and blood.[1]

How then, did I dare attempt a book on him? Not by choice I can assure you. I made several efforts to secure his time and attention—alas, all in vain.

When I began this project I was beseiged with 'is it a pro-Sanjay or anti-Sanjay book?' I tried to explain that it was neither, it was simply 'a book'. My reply was met with scepticism, some

---

1 Neither have I met Maneka.

went as far as to suggest that one couldn't write 'a book' on Sanjay Gandhi, it had to be one or the other.

Since I refused to be pigeon-holed, it was assumed, by the Sanjay camp at least, that the book would be hostile to him. The record of the magazine I edited did not help to dispel that belief.

I will not deny that during the Emergency I remained unimpressed by 'the new saviour', indeed in his creation and personality I saw the real evil of the Emergency. However, by the time I actually started working on the project I had come around to a sneaking sympathy for the man. There had been, or so it appeared, so much over-reaction and over-kill in the post election press that I was determined to stay clear of the charge of a 'loaded' book. For a start I decided I would not have chapter headings like: 'Dark side of the moon' or 'Night of the long knives'. One does not fight rhetoric with rhetoric.

I am not sure whether my book is 'sympathetic' or 'hostile' to Sanjay Gandhi, this is for others to judge; what I do know is that I tried with application and honesty to report and interpret facts as I uncovered them. And at all times I gave the benefit of doubt to Mr Gandhi. If unable to double check and confirm a story, I dropped it (I could write a book on the stories I dropped). In the charged atmosphere prevailing in the country no other course was open to me.

My original intention had been to tape long interviews with Sanjay and use them as a starting point for my research. By August '77, however, Sanjay was, or he thought he was, much harrassed and hounded by journalists. A spate of books on Mrs Gandhi's 21 months had hit the stands in which he appeared in the role of 'public enemy number one' (Sanjay's words). These books had enjoyed huge sales; another on the same subject could only add to his discomfiture.

True, my book was not on the Emergency. It would, however, by necessity cover aspects of it. Moreover, whereas the existing literature was not specifically Sanjay oriented, I was contemplating a book focused entirely on him. For a 'public enemy number one' already busy answering accusations from Uma Vasudev, Kuldip Nayar, Jannardhan Thakur, that was not a prospect to look forward to. In truth, I cannot blame him for avoiding me.

Meanwhile, I was given to understand that if I promised a pro-Sanjay stance I would have the full cooperation of 12, Willingdon Crescent. But how was I to prove—and proof was required— my pro-Sanjay stance? And what did pro-Sanjay mean? A whitewash job?

On my second visit to Delhi I wrote a letter to Sanjay, and sent it to him by hand. I informed him that I was writing a 'serious' book which would be sympathetic i.e. it would begin from a position of neutrality and examine all data on its merits. Would he see me? Mr Gandhi read the letter and uttered only two words: 'No chance.'

On a subsequent trip to the capital I rang up Maneka. We were both editors and I thought if nothing else we might have an opportunity to talk. I may have got the odd word wrong but the conversation went something like this.

'Surya? Can I speak to Maneka Gandhi please?... Hello Maneka?'

'Yes.'

'Maneka this is Vinod Mehta from Bombay.'

'Yes.'

'Well, I am here for a few days and I though we might meet.'

'Is it about your book?'

'Well, er, yes.'

'I am sorry, I don't want to meet you. And neither does Sanjay. Anything else, Mr Mehta?'

'Well, er, no.'

I repeated this conversation to Satindra Singh, a Delhi journalist and old friend. He said he would speak to Maneka. He did. I was given a number to ring in the evening. When I spoke a second time to her Maneka opened up. She told me how 'let down' Sanjay had been by others he had spoken to. I explained the background of my book; it would be objective. 'They all say that,' said Maneka. To prove my objectivity I reeled off a list of people I had met in Delhi, all of them from the Sanjay camp. 'I am listening to both sides' I said. Maneka was unimpressed. 'I believe you've already written half your book. Sanjay says he will see you only after he has seen what you have written.' Was he asking to vet my manuscript? 'Yes.'

I don't think any writer with any professional integrity could have accepted those conditions.

In a way I was relieved when I received this 'offer' from Sanjay, which was for me the final no. In the one or two interviews Mr Gandhi had given after the elections he had said things like: 'No coercion took place in the family planning programme.' How do you interview someone who, in the face of overwhelming evidence, denies everything? I could envisage a situation, if he had agreed to meet me, where I would ask questions and he would simply say 'no' or 'not true.' How would I incorporate his series of denials into my text?

I had also heard from Kuldip Nayar the kind of conditions Sanjay had imposed on him for the interview he gave Kuldip a week after the election results. They met in the lawns of 1, Safdarjang. Sanjay 'stood dazed under a tree', but he still insisted on no tape-recorder or notes during the interview; neither could anything he said be directly attributed to him.

I wish Sanjay had met me. Coming back from Dehradun I had bought his favourite Kwality toffees, which I hoped to present to him as a peace offering. Finally, I ate them all myself, not with any great relish I might add.

IN ANY CONVERSATION ON Sanjay Gandhi one is frequently asked: 'What is he like?' There is good reason for the frequency of this question. During the Emergency we were led to believe that he was the great redeemer, now we are told he is a fool, a charlatan. Understandably, there is some confusion about his real merits.

Let us begin with his intelligence, and straight away refute the popular impression that he is a fool. There is no evidence from Doon School to suggest that he was dim. There is a great deal of evidence from Doon to suggest that he was not interested in his studies, but that is not the same as being dim.

He could, on the other hand, handle difficult situations with cunning and guile. A week after the elections were announced, the Foreign Press Journalists Association of Delhi invited Sanjay to address a press conference. He came alone, without notes, and faced thirty, hard-bitten, crafty, hostile journalists for over an hour. I have a tape of that press conference, one in which the foreign scribes[2] tried consistently to trip him up, tried consistently to trap him into an indiscretion—but he did not oblige. 'It was,' as the Reuters man said later, 'a masterly performance. He was very impressive.'

Sanjay's followers eagerly point to his Five Point plan as an example of their hero's perspicacity and genius. To some extent they are justified in their claims, the Five-Point plan was 'brilliant', and one must grant Sanjay some credit for isolating India's more pressing problems. However, I am pretty sure that if you picked up a taxi-driver in any city of India, he would, with equal ease, facility and accuracy tell you what is wrong with the country. Too many mouths to feed, too few jobs, strikes, corruption, the stigma of caste distinction... Defining problems is easy in India, presenting solutions is not so easy.

Sanjay was not short on solutions, solutions which revealed the true nature of his intellect and imagination. Having defined population control as imperative, he sought to implement sterilization by terror and intimidation—if people were not coming voluntarily to the operating table, use force. Having defined slums as an urban ill, he sought to implement slum clearance by bulldozers—if people would not leave for the resettlement colonies, use force. Having defined law and order as essential 'to get development going', he sought to implement it by putting dissenters in jail—if someone had a different point of view he must be a traitor, so use force. Having defined the need for a 'positive press' he sought to implement that concept by cutting off government ads and electricity—if newspapers

---

2 The foreign journalists were gunning for Sanjay at this press conference in reprisal for the way Shukla had treated them.

criticized him they must be 'motivated', or worse, 'commies', so use force.

Consistent in this attitude is a frightening simplicity. Sanjay did not believe in greys, things were either black or white. He was incapable of grasping that while his aims in the family planning programmes were excellent, the task was of Byzantine complexity. There were historical, social, religious, political, economic implications in nasbandi, but to him all this was an excuse for lethargy and inactivity. Sanjay was really convinced, for instance, that the people of Turkman Gate would, after the initial shock, be grateful to him for demolishing their houses. 'Our strongest support in Delhi,' he declared while campaigning, 'will come from the people of the resettlement colonies.'

Intellectually Sanjay had never encountered complexity. He was an I.S.C. and at that educational level you are not likely to learn (through your educational training) the art of resolving involved problems. Moreover, once out of school, Sanjay never bothered to supplement his formal education. He himself confessed in 1976 that possibly his strongest intellectual stimulation came from comics.

Those who have met Sanjay confirm that he can be embarrassingly laconic. His brief, telegraphic answers to obtuse, intricate questions may have been a 'refreshing change' for some, but they were also very unrevealing. I think it was Karanjia who asked him whether he believed in 'Left or Right'. Mr Gandhi said he believed in 'whatever was good for the country'. This was immediately heralded as one more example of the young man's pragmatism and impatience with the 'snake pit of ideology'. Maybe, but I suspect that Sanjay didn't quite understand the question. His habit of reducing everything to its lowest common denominator characterized his approach to problem solving.

Thus Sanjay brought to bear on India's myriad and gigantic concerns an I.S.C. brain, one which in the course of a day might reflect and pronounce on tourism, industrial licensing, family planning, town beautification, state politics, dowry, harijans...

Sanjay was neither stupid nor intelligent. His mental capacities were on par with those of any average I.S.C. student. And I must confess I would be slightly uneasy if such a person was making India's most vital decisions. On the other hand I would have no objections to such a person running a restaurant or driving a bus.

When Sanjay was in power, alarm and surprise was expressed in some quarters at the kind of people he had gathered around him. Not for me. I find Sanjay's choice of mates and companions entirely consistent with his personality and intellectual inclinations. Possibly one or two of Sanjay's associates had better educational qualifications than him but their approach and attitude to problems was equivalent.

It is significant that Sanjay greatly distrusted intelligence in its conventional form. He had no time for experienced, senior civil servants or for someone like P. N. Haksar, possibly because they may have pointed out to him the realities of the world. He was also, I am sure, intellectually intimidated by them (he ousted a Kashmiri mafia to impose a Punjabi mafia). Meanwhile, Bansi Lal, R.K. Dhawan, Arjun Das, Jagmohan, Bhinder, Navin Chawla were on his wavelength, besides having one further qualification: they never queried orders. They knew that the order was paramount, how they executed it was their business. In Sanjay's world, ends not means received kudos.

So did Sanjay know about the means? In Delhi the excuse governing Sanjay's (and Mrs Gandhi's) insensitivity and savagery is based on the 'he did not know' theme. The 12, Willingdon Crescent people will tell you mournfully that the 'family has been destroyed by others.'

That may be so. But I think it is an insult to the intelligence of the Indian people for Sanjay or Mrs Gandhi, having perpetrated all manner of indignities on us, to plead ignorance as a justification. Sanjay knew precisely what was happening in the country. He knew what Jagmohan was doing, he knew what Bansi Lal was doing; indeed they were doing it under his instructions and with his blessings.

I have met many people who assure me that Sanjay is a kind and gentle person. He speaks softly, he does not lose his temper, he is polite and courteous. I myself know of a couple of examples of his generosity, all of which makes comprehension of his callousness and indifference to other people's suffering difficult. Sanjay was no sadist, no Attila the Hun, but once he had decided on a course of action he was ruthless. Example: he was determined to rid Delhi of slums and any resistance he met to that measure was mercilessly squashed. Cruelty was not integral to Sanjay's 'programme of national development', it was integral to the manner of its implementation. And he knew it.

When people are shy they usually have good reason for being so. Sanjay's munificent shyness is no exception. Like his mother he is seldom expansive, instead he is invariably guarded, hesitant. Surrounded by crowds and courtiers, as he was during the Emergency, he felt distinctly uncomfortable. Everywhere he went speeches had to be made, questions answered, media impression confirmed.

When Chief Ministers like Tewari or Shukla organized the elaborate 'tamashas' on his arrival in their state, Sanjay feigned annoyance at the waste of public moneys. This was cited as proof of his innate simplicity and distaste for pomp and show.

I don't think that is quite true. Sanjay's shyness is linked directly to his self-confidence. He was never sure if he was worthy of the 'crown', hence the need for the retinue of cheerleaders whose only job was to assure him that he was a colossal public figure. He knew, of course, that he was no colossal public figure; at best he hoped to acquire charisma along the way. So in a sense the arches, the bhangras, the rented crowds were necessary to sustain him. If Sanjay really abhorred the vulgar displays of phoney welcome he had only to snap his fingers and they would stop.

The real root of Sanjay's shyness was failure. All his life, in everything he attempted, he had failed—conspicuously. Despite having access to the best of opportunities, his entire career till 25 June 1975 was one short, sad list of defeats. He had failed as a student, he had failed as an apprentice, he had failed with women, he had failed with Maruti. In a family* of successes he stuck out like a sore thumb. If one has lived this series of failures one is, inevitably, going to be shy, one is going to lack self-confidence. Thus when people say Sanjay is shy what they are really saying is that he has no self-confidence. But how could he?

Once the Emergency had been called, Sanjay realized that he had a unique opportunity to correct his past. Now he was going to prove himself to all those who had ridiculed him as a failure. With one spectacular, speedy success—the salvation of India—he would wipe out his previous record. This was the motivation for the typhoon pace which characterized all of Sanjay's plans.

Population escalation had to be contained in one year, slums wiped out in a week, beggars removed overnight, strikes banned immediately. Sanjay gave himself less than a year to demonstrate to the nation, to his detractors and to himself that he was gifted too. Speed was also essential since he couldn't be certain when his mother would lift the Emergency, leaving him out in the cold.

Which leads us nicely to the relationship between mother and son, a relationship which has baffled, intrigued, exasperated national and international commentators. After acres of editorial and analytical coverage, after numerous books, opinion is still divided. 'Why did she allow him to do it?' is a question not he, only she can answer. The rest of us can take guesses.

Certainly during the latter part of the Emergency it became clear that we were watching the unfolding of a Greek tragedy, for sooner rather than later the boy was going to destroy her. Why did a woman credited with possibly the shrewdest political brain in the country, a person who loved power (indeed, it seemed the sole purpose of her existence), a Prime Minister who in the past had snuffed out even incipient contenders, allow herself to be humiliated and annihilated slowly but surely in front of her own eyes? Mr Costa Gavras who specializes in filming political mysteries has a ready-made subject here.

Four theories can be floated to explain the Indira-Sanjay connection, theories which cover pretty extensive ground, taking in the positions of 'those who loved her and those who hated her'. I enumerate them all, the more absurd first.

Incest. There is a lunatic fringe which finds this notion credible. This fringe presents pseudo-Freudian deductions to advance its prejudices. Without being prim, I think it is a preposterous assumption, one not worth expanding.

The second is blackmail. During the Emergency one heard various rumours of the 'hold' Sanjay exercised on his mother. It was said that he had a file implicating her in embezzlement; it was said that he had 'pictures' of her with lovers; it was said that Lalit Narain Misra and Sanjay together blackmailed Indira through documents Misra possesssed.

The 'hold' theory gained further respectability and currency when Lewis Symons of the *Washington Post* wrote in his paper that Sanjay had slapped his mother, not once, but six times—and in public. If he could get away with that, then surely he must have something on her was the general feeling then.

Lewis Symons's slapping story was widely published in the Indian press after the elections, and those who wanted to believe it believed it. I believe the story is false. Mr Symons has the reputation of being a sensationalist and 'a bit of a shit' (the words of a foreign correspondent who knew him in Delhi). Symons has to date not revealed his source. When did Sanjay slap his mother? Where did he slap her? At what public occasion? Who else was present? Who was doing the counting? My own view is that Symons fell upon a cocktail party anecdote and mistook it for the truth.

The reality is that Sanjay has seldom 'raised his voice' to Indira, and Indira has seldom 'raised her voice' to Sanjay. Fertile imaginations saw long, heated arguments at 1, Safdarjang between mother and son once the results came in and once it became clear who was to blame. In fact there have been no arguments—hot or cold. 'Mrs Gandhi has never spoken a harsh word to Sanjay after the election. I am sure she knows who is to blame, but if you know anything about her then you know she hates displays of emotion' says a Gandhi watcher.

If anything, Mrs Gandhi has become even more concerned and protective towards her son. (Note her stubborn refusal to denounce him or even mildly criticize his role despite pleas from friends and party workers. Instead she constantly defends him and his programmes.)

Three days after Congress lost, the Gandhi family sat for their mid-day meal. It was—as always—a simple lunch: dal and karelas. During the meal Mrs Gandhi glanced at Sanjay's plate to notice he was eating his chappatis with dal alone. And then she remembered: Sanjay did not like karelas. She flew into a rage. The cook was summoned. 'Don't you know Sanjay does not eat karelas? Why do you make vegetables he doesn't like?' she thundered. The cook apologized, promised never to repeat his mistake and retreated trembling. That is not the kind of concern shown by a mother who holds a 'grudge' against her son.

Sanjay has no file on his mother, neither did he blackmail her.

The third theory concerns faith and respect for political wisdom. During 'the dark days' of the Allahabad High Court trial, Sanjay stood by his mother. Subsequently when she was universally advised to 'step down' he advised her to fight it out. Moreover, as I discussed in an earlier chapter, the imposition of the Emergency was such an unqualified success (from the Congress point of view) that Mrs Gandhi was beholden to Sanjay not only for his moral support but for his political presence too.

The third theory, thus, partially explains the Sanjay-Indira connection.

It cannot, however, be the full explanation, for as the Emergency progressed Mrs Gandhi was fully aware of her son's deeds. She had, in fact, developed a set response to complaints about her son. She would listen uneasily without speaking a word or asking a question. When the person had finished his tale of woe she would say thank you and call the meeting to a close. She never indicated if she would make enquiries or confirm or take corrective action.

We now come to the final theory. It is the one I favour, indeed, in my view, it is the key to the riddle. I am afraid it is not overly sophisticated or polished, neither is it likely to appeal to those with a fondness for the sinister and an aversion to the simplistic.

Mrs Gandhi permitted her son to do all the things he did during the Emergency because he was her son. Period.

I accept that filial devotion is a bit of a let down as 'the clue' to the connection. But it is possibly a useful corrective to the masculine Indira Gandhi image—remember 'the only man'?—secure in the country. This tough, wily, calculating politician, who was supposed to have suppressed her natural character for high public office, turned out, as far as her younger son was concerned, to be just another mother, more accurately an Indian mother. Accordingly, as Vijaya Lakshmi Pandit pointed out, he was her 'Achilles heel'.

I am certain that in Sanjay's case Mrs Gandhi suffered from feelings of guilt. She knew he was the product of a broken home, she knew he was greatly attached to her, yet she had been unable to fulfil her conventional mother role because of her 'duty to the nation'. Sanjay had always been mummy's boy, but mummy was seldom around. Was this the reason he had turned out to be 'difficult'? Nurtured in a happier family environment, would he have emerged normal?

Like any mother who realizes late in her life that she is guilty of neglect, she allowed her son freedoms and liberties which other mothers would have granted hesitantly. In compensating, she over-compensated,

For example, nobody has ever heard or seen Indira contradict Sanjay. 'It is an accepted fact in the household that Sanjay knows best,' says a close family friend. Since the mother refused to correct her son, others followed suit. During the Emergency, Sanjay was never open to suggestions or ideas simply because 'he knew best'. No matter what the subject he was an authority, and thus inflexible. The others were there merely to concur. On the rare occasion when someone did venture to offer a different point of view Sanjay would say: 'You think about it again.'

The one person who contested Sanjay's infallibility was Rajiv—but only when he was provoked. A few months after Sanjay had begun his flying lessons he fell into an argument with Rajiv— already a pilot of long standing—on some technical point relating to aviation. Surrounded by half a dozen pilots at the Delhi Flying club Sanjay insisted he was right while his brother was wrong. Exasperated, Rajiv finally asked sardonically: 'Sanjay, how long have you been flying?'

For some inexplicable reason in this part of the world, sons of prime ministers and presidents have taken a heavy toll on their parents. Ayub Khan's sons wrought havoc in Pakistan, Mrs Bandaranaike's son openly confessed that he took inspiration from Sanjay, Mr Jagjivan Ram's son has caused the father much embarrassment, and currently Morarjee Desai's son says 'he is biding his time'. Strong, powerful and assertive politicians become weak, cringing and helpless when confronted with their sons. Mrs Gandhi might draw some comfort from that.

At the time of writing, Mr Sanjay Gandhi is still a free bird. He boasts that he is 'innocent' and is determined to stay on in India to prove it. Those who have seen and spoken to him recently say that he 'is on top of the world'. It is incredible how normal and relaxed he is when you consider the kind of pressure he must be under. Sanjay has put on a little weight, he goes to his factory every morning 'because it is something to do' and in the afternoon he plays with his dogs, and badminton with his wife. He jokes that he is 'public enemy number one—but I'll get over it. They have nothing against me. At the most I will have to pay a fine of Rs. 500 and my Company Secretary may get into trouble.'

If I was Sanjay I wouldn't be so sure. Since he was involved with almost every aspect of Emergency activity and since most of these are currently under public scrutiny, both he and his Company Secretary might be in very serious trouble. No doubt most of the 'dastardly deeds' were ordered on the telephone (indeed, the entire Emergency seems to have been implemented and coordinated either verbally or through the phone), so little paper evidence exists—a situation which helps keep Sanjay out of prison. However, I refuse to believe that in those hectic 21 months Sanjay did not drop his guard once. Considering the magnitude and variety of his 'excesses', there must be some scrap of paper which will indict him. The public enemy number one will have to be phenomenally lucky to get away.

It is enormously tempting for this writer to conclude that there are various and profound lessons to be learnt from the rise and fall of Sanjay Gandhi. (If you have slaved over a book for eight months the temptation is almost irresistible.) I do not wish to deny the import of the Sanjay phenomenon; neither do I wish to manufacture synthetic moral lessons.

If there is a lesson—and in my judgement there is only one— it is that right across the spectrum there exists in India a latent streak of 'sycophancy' capable of surfacing at the behest of the likes of Indira, Sanjay and God knows who else. The police constable and the senior civil servant shed with extraordinary ease not philosophical concepts like integrity or 'dictates of conscience' but the everyday dos and donts of their profession. I know—as I am so often reminded—that these people had families to support, daughters to marry, sons to educate and L.I.C. premiums to pay.

But India required no martyrs, it needed people who would stand up for rather simple organizational standards. If the four editors of the four major national dailies had spurned Shukla's commands not because of opposition to the Emergency but because their papers could not 'work' under those strictures, could censorship have been imposed so serenely? Did any D.I.G. or I.G. ask for written orders? Was there any minister who refused to discuss government policy with Sanjay on grounds of security?

There are, of course, individual instances of exemplary courage. Alas, they are few and far between. The majority acquiesced, indeed revelled in their acquiescence. I am told by friends, more learned than myself, that in the late 30s and early 40s Germany witnessed a similar degree of sycophancy and silence. The analogy is specious. Mrs Gandhi and her son had no concentration camps, and India was not at war. Sanjay did not only reveal himself during the Emergency, he revealed aspects of our national character. In a sense he has done us a service, I only hope we are wiser for the experience.

Had Sanjay (and his mother) possessed more finesse, had he not been in such a tearing hurry, had he been slightly more intelligent, he would have become 'the national leader' he so desperately wished to be. Was it a small miscalculation—the elections—of his mother that let us off the hook so easily?

Alarmists construct a scenario in which Sanjay could make a 'come back'. Despite the hazards of political punditry, I am prepared to give long odds against that possibility. Even if he escapes going to jail, Sanjay Gandhi's political career appears permanently concluded.

The Sanjay Story is really nothing but a rather squalid and commonplace tale of nepotism and opportunism. Privately, I suspect, Mr Gandhi would agree with that assessment.

Bibliography

(Books only)

Abbas Khwaja, Ahmad. *Indira Gandhi: Return of the Red Rose* (Popular Prakashan, Bombay, 1966)

Abbas Khwaja, Ahmad. *That Woman* (Orient Paperbacks, Delhi, 1973)

Bhargava, G.S.. *Indira's India Gate* (Arnold Heineman, Delhi, 1975)

Bhatia, Krishan. *Indira Gandhi* (Angus Robertson, London, 1974)

Bose and Dayal. *Delhi Under Emergency* (ESS Publications, Delhi, 1977)

Bright, J.S.. *Indira Gandhi* (New Light, Delhi, 1975)

Drieberg, Trevor. *Profile in Courage: Indira Gandhi* (Vikas, Delhi, 1973)

Brecher, Michael. *Nehru: A Political Biography* (Oxford, London, 1959)

Desai, Bhadra. *Indira Gandhi* (Popular Prakashan, Bombay, 1966)

Gandhi, Indira. *Selected Speeches* (Publications Division, Delhi, 1971)

George, T. J. S.. *Krishna Menon* (Jaico, Bombay, 1964)

Hutheesing, Krishna. *With No Regrets* (Padma Publications, Bombay, 1944)

Hutheesing, Krishna. *Dear To Behold* (Pearl I.B.H., Bombay, 1969)

Kalhan, Promilla. *Kamala Nehru* (Vikas, Delhi, 1973)

Kalhan, Promilla. *Black Wednesday* (Sterling, Delhi, 1977)

Kulkarni, V. B.. *My Country and My Rulers* (Jaico, Bombay, 1977)

Mankekar, Kamala and D. R.. *Decline and Fall of Indira Gandhi* (Vision, Delhi, 1977)

Moraes, Dom. *A Matter of People* (Andre Deutsch, London, 1974)

Moraes, Frank. *Indira Gandhi* (D.A.V.P., Delhi, 1966)

Moraes, Frank. *Jawaharlal Nehru* (Jaico, Bombay, 1959)

Murthy, R. K.. *The Cult of the Individual* (Sterling, Delhi, 1977)

Nanda, B. R.. *The Nehrus: Motilal and Jawaharlal* (George Alien and Unwin, London, 1962)

Nayar, Kuldip. *The Judgement* (Vikas, Delhi, 1977)

Nehru, Jawaharlal. *An Autobiography* (Allied, Bombay, 1962)

Nehru, Jawaharlal. *Discovery of India* (Meridan, London, 1960)

Puri, Rajinder. *India 1969-75, The Wasted Years* (Chetna, Delhi, 1975)

Rau, Chalapathi: (ed.). *Indira Priyadarshni* (Popular, Delhi, 1966)

Sahgal, Nayantara. *Prison and Chocolate Cake* (Victor Gollancz, London, 1954)

Sahni, N. C.. *Indira* (Sterling, Delhi, 1967)

Sen, Ella. *Indira Gandhi* (Rupa, Calcutta, 1973)

Selbourne, David. *An Eye to India* (Pelican Books, London, 1977)

Sinha, B. M.. *Operation Emergency* (Hindi, Delhi, 1977)

Thakur, Janardhan. *All the Prime Minister's Men* (Vikas, Delhi, 1977)

Vasudev, Uma. *Indira Gandhi* (Vikas, Delhi, 1974)

Vasudev, Uma. *Two Faces of Indira Gandhi* (Vikas, Delhi, 1977)

Index